# A-LEVEL YEAR 2

## STUDENT GUIDE

## OCR

# Sociology

## Debates in contemporary society

Globalisation and the digital social world
Option 2: Education

Steve Chapman, Lesley Connor and
Katherine Roberts

**HODDER**
EDUCATION
AN HACHETTE UK COMPANY

Hodder Education, an Hachette UK company, Blenheim Court, George Street, Banbury, Oxfordshire OX16 5BH

*Orders*

Bookpoint Ltd, 130 Milton Park, Abingdon, Oxfordshire OX14 4SB

tel: 01235 827827

fax: 01235 400401

email: education@bookpoint.co.uk

Lines are open 9.00 a.m.–5.00 p.m., Monday to Saturday, with a 24-hour message answering service. You can also order through the Hodder Education website: www.hoddereducation.co.uk

© Steve Chapman, Lesley Connor and Katherine Roberts 2017

ISBN 978-1-4718-5975-5

First printed 2017

Impression number 5 4 3 2 1

Year 2021 2020 2019 2018 2017

This Guide has been written specifically to support students preparing for the OCR A-level Sociology examinations. The content has been neither approved nor endorsed by OCR and remains the sole responsibility of the authors.

Typeset by Integra Software Services Pvt. Ltd., Pondicherry, India

Printed in Italy

Cover photo: thakala/Fotolia

Hachette UK's policy is to use papers that are natural, renewable and recyclable products and made from wood grown in sustainable forests. The logging and manufacturing processes are expected to conform to the environmental regulations of the country of origin.

# Contents

# ■ Getting the most from this book

Exam-style questions

Commentary on the questions

Tips on what you need to do to gain full marks, indicated by the icon 🄮

Sample student answers

Practise the questions, then look at the student answers that follow.

Commentary on sample student answers

Read the comments (preceded by the icon 🄮) showing how many marks each answer would be awarded in the exam and exactly where marks are gained or lost.

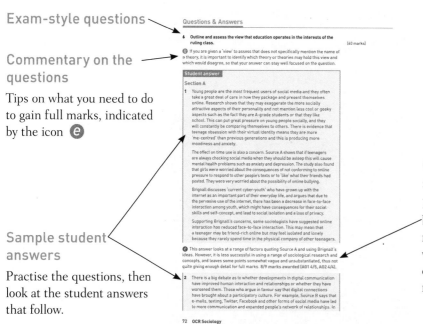

# ■ About this book

This guide covers Component 3: Debates in contemporary society in the OCR A-level Sociology specification H580. It focuses on the compulsory topic Globalisation and the digital social world and the optional topic Education.

## How to use the book

The first main section of the book is **Content Guidance**. It follows the headings for Debates in contemporary society in the OCR specification, specifically the topics Globalisation and the digital social world and Education. Each section of the Content Guidance contains exam tips, knowledge checks and definitions of key terms. Knowing and understanding the meaning of sociological concepts is an essential part of the whole course.

The second main section of the book is **Questions & Answers**. At the beginning of this section is information about the A-level examination and the different sections of the exam paper for this component. The A-level questions provided are in the style of the OCR exam for Component 3 and are each followed by an A-grade answer. Following each student answer you will find comments explaining why what has been written is good and is scoring well. More detailed guidance on how to use the Questions & Answers section is given at the beginning of that section.

# Content Guidance

## Section A Globalisation and the digital social world

### What is the relationship between globalisation and digital forms of communication?

#### Definitions of globalisation

Al-Rodhan (2015) points out that defining globalisation is anything but easy, while Ellwood describes the concept as 'the least understood concept of the new millennium'.

In 1964, Marshall McLuhan predicted the emergence of what he called the 'global village'. He likened communications and media in the 1960s to a giant central nervous system which ultimately would connect everybody in the world. He argued that this would eventually compress the world's thousands of cultures into one 'super-culture', predicting cultural homogenisation — the idea that cultural diversity would eventually be replaced by cultural sameness. McLuhan's idea of the global village can clearly be seen in modern definitions of globalisation.

Albrow, for example, defines globalisation as all those processes by which the disparate people of the world have been incorporated into a single society, while Waters observes that it is a social process in which the constraints of geography on economic, political, social and cultural arrangements have declined. At its simplest, globalisation means that the world we live in now feels smaller and more accessible than it was a decade ago.

Martell observes that, at a micro level, globalisation for individuals means that both geographical distance and time zones are no longer important. Harvey (1990) calls this space–time compression. The instantaneous interaction afforded by digital technology such as e-mails or instant messaging has erased distance and substituted virtual space for physical space. It doesn't matter where physically people are in the world; this global digital interconnectedness means people can occupy the same online space at the same time.

At a macro or societal level, globalisation means that goods, money, people, services, popular culture, drugs, crime, terror, disease, news, images, ideas, religions and pollution are now crossing national borders on an extraordinary scale and at an incredible speed. Societies that were once distant, independent and very different to one another, are today increasingly globally intertwined and interdependent whether they want to be or not. Moreover, the macro and micro are also interwoven in that the local lives of ordinary people everywhere in the world are increasingly shaped by events, decisions and actions that take place thousands of miles from where they live and work.

**Exam tip**

The examiner expects you to be aware of the various definitions of globalisation and to consider the problems in defining the concept.

**Cultural homogenisation** Refers to the reduction in cultural diversity across the world and its replacement with cultural sameness, especially in popular culture. A homogeneous world is one composed of elements that are all of the same kind or essentially alike. It is based on the idea that the more people consume the same films, music and brands, the more likely they are to feel connected despite distance. There may be a sense of global community based on similar cultural experience which may have the long-term effect of reducing cultural diversity.

**Knowledge check 1**

Explain what is meant by space–time compression.

## The emergence of globalisation

Sociologists who argue in favour of globalisation argue that it has been brought about by the following.

### Technological advances

Advances in digital forms of communication and computer technology, particularly e-mail, smartphones, satellite technology, digital television, texting and the internet (with its diversity of websites, social media networks and blogs), have transformed the world's concept of time, distance and space. Information in all its varied forms — news, political ideas and dissent, financial transactions and cultural products — can now be transmitted instantaneously to most global destinations from any part of the world that has a digital connection. For example, most banks, stock exchanges and trading markets have utilised digital technology to set up a 24-hour global financial market, while transnational businesses have used digital technology such as e-mails, conference calls and the internet to effectively manage an international division of labour in which production and marketing are often scattered across continents.

Digital communications have helped to globalise war, conflict and terrorism. For example, smartphones in Africa are seen as necessities in coordinating civil wars, while terrorist organisations such as al-Qaeda and ISIS have successfully used the internet and social networking sites to globally publicise their cause.

### Ownership and control of digital media

Ownership and control of the world's digital forms of communication have become increasingly concentrated in the hands of fewer transnational corporations. This has resulted in cultural products such as films, television, music, designer fashion, news, social networking sites, food, drink, brands and sport being developed and manufactured for global rather than local consumption. Steven (2004) observes that, despite huge differences in distance and upbringing, much of the world's population now listens to the same music and watches the same films and television via the same digital communication networks and social media.

### Other developments

Other important developments which may have contributed to a process of globalisation include the rapid growth of cheap air travel and mass tourism, as well as the continuing dominance of the English language in digital communication, particularly on the internet.

# Developments in digital forms of communication in a global society

## Digital revolution

Some sociologists argue that the social world can be divided into three revolutionary periods:

1   The agricultural revolution — the development of farming to cultivate crops.
2   The industrial revolution — the development of science and technology to build machinery in order to manufacture goods from raw materials in factories.

---

**Exam tip**

The micro–macro distinction is a useful evaluative tool. Don't just focus on the impact of globalisation on societies. Think also about its impact on individuals. For example, compare the impact of globalisation on your own life compared with someone living in a developing country.

---

**Knowledge check 2**

Identify three major reasons why some sociologists believe globalisation has occurred.

---

3 The computer or information age — the development of the internet or worldwide web. This global multimedia library of information and services in cyberspace is made possible by a global system of interconnected super-computers. The development of high-capacity broadband wireless networks means more people than ever can connect at high speed to this super-information highway and communicate in forms very different to those found in the pre-digital age such as physically chatting with a friend, talking on the telephone, sending a fax or writing a letter. For example, Skype means that users can see and chat to other people on the other side of the world.

The early twenty-first century saw a further revolution in communication as society entered a digital age. Digitalisation refers to a dramatic change in the way information is stored and transmitted. All information, regardless of format (for example, images, text and sound) is now converted into binary code. This led to an explosion of new types of digital communication devices including cheap laptop computers, tablets, smartphones and digital television.

Digitalisation led to three types of **media convergence**:

- **Technological convergence** refers to the fact that digitalisation has led to the merging of different types of information — text, photographs, video, film, voices, maps, e-mail, music and social networking — into a single delivery system or digital communication device such as smart televisions, laptops, tablets and smartphones. Digitalisation now allows information to be delivered immediately across a range of media platforms which were once separate and unconnected technologies.

- **Economic convergence** refers to the fact that media, computer, television and telecommunications companies that once operated in separate spheres of development and production are increasingly engaging in technological and economic alliances with one another to produce multimedia delivery systems. This is because digitalisation has rendered the borders between these forms of communication irrelevant.

- **Cultural convergence** refers to the fact that most members of society increasingly interact with one another using the same type of digital communication. Old ways of communicating such as writing letters are gradually being replaced by digital social media networks such as Facebook, Snapchat, Instagram and Twitter. Cultural convergence means that the way people consume is changing too. For example, six out of ten British adults now use the internet to buy products such as food, clothing, music, insurance and holidays.

A major feature of the digital age has been the appearance and rapid spread of social media platforms. Social media refers to a participatory culture or network of websites and applications which enable a community of users to interact and collaborate. This participatory culture enables users to create and share content, to engage in social networking and to spread news. There are different types of social media, for example:

- Digital social networks, which encourage registered users to create public profiles and make lists of users who can be invited to share connections, upload photos and videos, send messages and keep in touch with friends, family and colleagues via computers, tablets and smartphones.

**Exam tip**

It is important not to judge the pre-digital era as inferior. It is merely different and can be used to evaluate the importance of digital media. For example, are old forms of media such as newspapers and television really redundant?

The most popular social networking site in the world is Facebook. In the USA, web users spend more time on Facebook than any other website, while in the UK Facebook is the default setting for 96% of adults who are online, according to a 2014 Ofcom survey. According to its official ethos, Facebook aims to make the world a more connected, open and empathetic place by encouraging people to share their social profile (identity and status), interests, feelings and so on and to maximise connectedness by accumulating friends and likes.

- Microblogging sites such as Twitter, which has 500 million users worldwide.
- Sites run by individual diarists and commentators known as bloggers, who write about a diversity of subjects from baking to politics.
- Video bloggers or vloggers, who upload videos of themselves onto YouTube, discussing commercial products relating to beauty or fashion, for example. Many of these are sponsored by advertisers.
- Open content sites such as Wikipedia, on which users are encouraged to collaborate on an online web encyclopaedia.
- Social news forums such as Reddit, on which stories are socially curated, promoted and discussed by site members.
- Global conference sites such as TED talks, which are devoted to spreading academic ideas.
- Virtual-world sites such as CyberCity, Second Life and World of Warcraft, which enable users to live alternative lives in alternative virtual worlds. For example, Second Life has over a million global users. Participants create virtual 3-D representations of themselves called avatars, who are able to interact, socialise, trade and even have sex with other avatars.

Before the computer/digital age, people who wished to share their interests, ideas or opinions with people in other parts of the country or world were constrained by geographical distance, time zones and forms of communication that were either slow (letters) or expensive (telephones). However, the computer/digital age has produced **virtual communities** in which globally dispersed people with common interests are no longer constrained by geographical distance or time zones. The existence of the internet and its diversity of websites, newsgroups, discussion boards, social networking platforms and so on, as well as e-mail and video applications such as Skype, has produced instantaneous interaction and sharing at any time and from any place.

**Virtual communities**
Communities that exist on the internet.

Van Dijk argues that both identity and community are increasingly shaped by these virtual communities. For example, he observes that teenagers can no longer imagine organising their social lives without Facebook at its centre; news organisations have become increasingly dependent on Twitter for breaking news stories; would-be pop superstars ignore YouTube at their peril, while A-level students cannot imagine an academic world without Google and Wikipedia. Carter argues that members of virtual communities see the relationships that they establish online as equally important to those that they establish in offline physical communities.

## Networked global society

This concept is mainly associated with the Marxist sociologist Manuel Castells, who argued that in the twenty-first century people are more likely to be organised into horizontal digital communication networks using new forms of social media than in the traditional vertical organisations of the past. Moreover, these networks connect people and allow them to be interactive at the speed of light. Digital technologies have therefore transformed all relationships whether they are personal, political, religious, cultural or economic.

For example, politics used to involve either joining vertical organisations such as a political party or pressure group and/or reading the products of such organisations, for example political manifestos. In addition, media organisations, which were also vertical organisations, attempted to influence voters. Consequently, political news or scandal travelled relatively slowly.

However, in contrast, Castells argues that new digital media such as Twitter, Facebook, blogs and websites have transformed not only the relationship that the electorate now has with politicians but also the way that politicians now behave — political news and gossip is instantaneously available via these new media networks and can ruin political careers within minutes. Moreover, these networks are global too, so people's political interests now often extend beyond domestic politics to how Britain engages with the rest of the world.

## Applying sociological theories to digital forms of communication

### Marxism

Marxist ideas about digital and social media constitute a critical digital sociology. Fuchs, for example, generally takes a conflict view of the role of digital communication in reproducing and legitimating inequality in capitalist society.

Fuchs observes that Karl Marx argued that 'the ideas of the ruling class are in every epoch the ruling ideas … The class which has the means of material production at its disposal, has control at the same time over the means of mental production, so … the ideas of those who lack the means of mental production are subject to it.' Marxist theories of the media and the newer digitalised forms of communication therefore generally argue that all forms of communication are ideological in that they function on behalf of the capitalist ruling class to reproduce and justify class inequality. Marxists believe that the role of digital social media (along with other ideological agencies, such as traditional media, education and religion) is to bring about a state of 'false class consciousness' so that citizens do not criticise or challenge the unequal and unjust organisation of capitalist society.

Marxists argue that the popularity of social media such as Facebook functions to reinforce false class consciousness because digital social networks mainly focus on non-critical issues such as identity, entertainment and consumption, and consequently are rarely important vehicles of protest and social change. Those who own or control these new forms of communication and social networks aim to shape and manipulate how people think about the world they live in so that they only get a narrow range of 'approved' views and knowledge, with the result that 'alternative' and critical points of view are rarely heard or are dismissed altogether as extremist.

Seabrook sees the globalisation linked to digital communication as a type of **cultural imperialism** because it is dominated by Western cultural industries which use digital forms of communication to impose their cultural values on the rest of the world. He argues that integration into a single global economy and culture is a 'declaration of

---

**Knowledge check 3**

Explain the difference between a traditional vertical organisation and a horizontal digital network, using religion as the context.

**Exam tip**

Although the specification is not specifically asking you to explore theories such as functionalism, the New Right and interactionism, it is still useful to think about how these theories would interpret new forms of digital communication. You could use them as evaluation of Marxist, feminist and postmodernist theories.

**Knowledge check 4**

What do Marxists mean when they say all forms of digital communication are ideological?

**Cultural imperialism** Refers to the ability of richer nations and some global corporations to impose their cultural products on the rest of the world. It is often argued that cultural imperialism leads to cultural homogenisation.

cultural war' upon other cultures. It implies that traditional cultures have little or no value. Seabrook argues that this cultural imperialism attempts to replace diversity with homogenisation and this often results in painful social and religious disruption as local cultures attempt to resist. Some observers have suggested that the recent growth in Islamist fundamentalism may be a reaction to these processes.

Marxists often point to six factors which they claim support their case:

1  Digital forms of communication are merely a continuation of older forms of media and consequently are subject to the same economic and social influences. Cornford and Robins (1999) argue that the so-called new media are not that 'new'. Older forms of technology such as telephone landlines are still integral to the use of new digital communication, for example broadband connections to the internet. They argue that the only thing that is new about digital media is speed — information, news and entertainment can be accessed in 'real time'. Cornford and Robins suggest that what the new technologies permit is the refinement, extension and embellishment of traditional media.

2  Jenkins argues that most new forms of digital media have developed as a result of investment by the big media corporations and consequently ownership of digital communications is concentrated in the hands of a few major transnational corporations. In particular, he argues that owning different types of media made it more desirable for companies to develop content across a variety of media platforms and delivery systems. As Jenkins notes, 'digitalisation set the conditions for convergence; corporate conglomerates created its imperative'.

An examination of the internet suggests that it is dominated by a small number of media corporations — for example, Microsoft has developed most of the software required for accessing the net, while Google is the most popular search engine. Apple and Samsung dominate the smartphone market. Most of the internet's commercially viable content is therefore controlled and/or commissioned by a handful of media conglomerates.

3  Digital forms of communication are becoming increasingly commercialised. In particular, in the last 10 years there has been a major shift in internet activities, from educational use to commercial use. Advertising has become a central feature of most social networking sites. Technologies such as **cookies** can monitor and process the data generated by interactive media usage, so they can segment and target potential future audiences, and thus enhance profits.

4  Marxists such as Fuchs point out that those who participate in the new digital culture are not created equal. Corporations, governments — and even individuals within corporate media — exert greater power than aggregates of consumers or those with genuine political and economic grievances. They suggest that digital technologies and networks mainly strengthen the power of existing elites and, in so doing, they contribute to the 'muting' of those — the politically and economically repressed — who have genuine grievances with the way capitalism is organised.

**Knowledge check 5**

Why do Cornford and Robins argue that new forms of digital media are not that new?

**Cookie** Information that a website puts on your computer hard drive so that it can remember something about you at a later time.

**Knowledge check 6**

What do Marxists mean by 'muting'?

5 Castells has highlighted the global criminal economy, which overlaps with the legitimate global economy. It is worth at least £1 trillion a year and has been made possible by digital forms of communication.

6 Marxist critical thinkers such as McChesney highlight the similarity of digital content and social networking. Facebook, Google and Twitter, for example, operate in hundreds of countries across the world. McChesney claims such companies are like imperial powers colonising the minds of millions of people across the world so they behave and think in the same way. He argues that this 'cult of homogeneity', which speaks to everyone in general and no one in particular, crowds out local cultural products. He claims that it has also reduced people's opportunity to speak out, that is, it has silenced or muted less powerful groups so that they are less likely to challenge issues such as inequality or to speak out against injustice.

**Exam tip**

Think about using examples of the types of global crime that might be facilitated by digital communication — for example, identity theft, tax fraud, pornography and terrorism.

However, this Marxist account of digital communications has been challenged for the following reasons.

- It assumes a unified conspiracy on the part of the providers of digital forms of communication. However, the owners of digital forms of communication are not united because their companies are involved in competition with one another for a bigger share of the market and therefore profit.

- Marxists tend to overemphasise social class at the expense of other inequalities that may also result in **muted voices** such as those relating to ethnicity, gender and sexuality.

- Neo-Marxists argue that ideas can exist independently of capitalism — these are not always the ideas of the ruling class and consequently do not always have to be ideological. Some Marxist observers of digital communications such as Castells have therefore argued that new media technologies and networks can revitalise democracy. It is argued that because the internet enables 'many to many' communication, it is capable of giving a voice to 'muted' groups such as the poor, the politically repressed, women, ethnic minorities, disabled people and the LGBT community, and encouraging greater community involvement in political action. It therefore gives a voice to those who would otherwise go unheard. It gives oppressed people the ability to come together and facilitate social change.

**Muted voices** Powerless social groups who are repressed or exploited. They are often prevented from speaking out and voicing their concerns.

## Feminism

Feminist theory has traditionally focused on how societies tend to be organised in patriarchal ways, that is, in favour of men. Males dominate positions of power in most societies and consequently women in contrast generally occupy subordinate positions.

Feminists are usually critical of both old media and digital forms of communication, which they see as patriarchal agencies which mainly engage in the symbolic annihilation of women, that is, they tend to show women in a narrow and limited range of social roles and to suggest that their achievements are less important than their looks and bodies. A good example of this with regard to digital communication is the popularity of pornography websites on the internet. Feminists also point out that control of the content of new digital forms of communication is in the hands of transnational corporations mainly owned by men.

**Knowledge check 7**

Why are feminists critical of both old media and digital forms of communication?

Feminists were responsible for the development of 'muted group theory', which suggests groups with little power or status are muted or silenced by more powerful groups. Feminists argued that women were often unable to voice their concerns about patriarchy because a male-dominated media suppressed or muted them. Kramarae extended this argument to the internet, which, she observes, is constructed and mainly controlled by men despite the fact that women use it as much as men do. She argues that the companies controlling the digital technology that underpins cybercommunication, the way the internet is organised, much of its software and even the metaphors used to describe the internet such as the 'super-information highway' are masculine and that this has the effect of 'muting' the voice of women.

**Knowledge check 8**

Who controls the internet, according to Kramarae?

However, some feminists are positive about the power of digital forms of communication to change women's social position in society for the better. Haraway argues that the anonymity granted by many forms of digital communication allows people to transcend an oppressed identity such as being female and to take on an alternative identity which avoids the negative judgements and stereotypes often applied to feminine identity. Internet and chat-room IDs and blog names can be asexual. The online visual community Second Life, in which users create a utopian world, is a particularly good example of how people might transcend their gender identity. Users construct an avatar — an image that represents them — from a selection of generic choices including buff male bodies, voluptuous female forms and asexual humanoid alternatives such as **cyborgs**. Sociological research on Second Life users suggests they do not feel limited by their real gender identities when choosing an avatar identity. For example, some women reported that they had deliberately chosen to adopt male bodies in order to experience a masculine identity, while other women preferred the cyborg identity because interaction with others excluded sexual politics.

**Cyborg** In the context of digital communications, refers to a gender-neutral cyber-identity.

Cochrane identifies a fourth wave of feminism which, she argues, is powered by digital technology which is encouraging women to build an empowering, popular and reactive feminist movement online. In other words, women's voices are no longer muted. Green and Singleton argue that digital technology and particularly the internet is a feminine technology that has the potential to destabilise patriarchy because its use allows women to explore, subvert and create new identities and to resist sexist representations wherever they might occur. A good example of this online empowerment is Laura Bates's 'Everyday Sexism' project, which in 2015 had 108,000 followers on Twitter and Facebook. This is a consciousness-raising initiative which encourages women to send in their everyday experiences of street harassment, sexual harassment especially on public transport, workplace discrimination and the **body shaming** that they encounter.

**Body shaming** Refers to criticising individuals (usually women) because they do not conform to 'ideal' body shapes as defined by men, for example, women may be shamed for being 'fat'.

Cochrane observes that women are using digital forms of communication to protest about pornography, page 3 of *The Sun* newspaper, violence against women, the sexualisation of childhood and so on. Cochrane argues that digital technology has resulted in contemporary young women adopting an 'intersectional' form of feminism in which they are aware of how multiple oppressions — class inequality, poverty, race, age, sexuality, gender, ability, violence and so on — intersect to bring about **misogyny** and patriarchal institutions.

**Knowledge check 9**

What is an intersectional form of feminism?

Green and Singleton emphasise the central use of the smartphone and particularly texting in the creation and maintenance of feminine identities, friendship networks and communities across local and global spaces.

**Misogyny** Refers to dislike or hatred of women.

However, evidence suggests that women who use digital forms of communication may still be subjected to sexism, abuse and threats. For example, women who use new media such as the internet may experience the sorts of everyday sexism experienced in older forms of media. For example, women's rights campaigner Caroline Criado-Perez was subjected to online rape and murder threats in 2013, while the academic Mary Beard and the MP Stella Creasy have also received threats and sexist abuse via Twitter. The internet may help disseminate feminist ideas more widely but it also does the same for its polar opposite — woman-hating views.

Some critics have also argued that the fourth wave of digital feminism might be exaggerated in terms of its influence on women. Moreover, Green and Singleton suggest that the online communities that are most popular with women users — Mumsnet and Facebook — might merely reinforce the patriarchal notion that women should perform the emotional work of maintaining family relationships.

## Postmodernism

Postmodernists see digital forms of communication as beneficial because they argue that global digital networks are primarily responsible for diffusing different cultural styles around the world and creating new global hybrid styles in fashion, food, music, consumption and lifestyle. It is argued that in the postmodern world this cultural diversity will become the global norm. Postmodernists therefore see globalisation as a positive phenomenon because it has created a new class of global consumers, in both the developed and the developing world, with a greater range of choices from which they can construct a **hybridised global identity**.

Postmodernists make the following claims.

- Postmodern societies are media-saturated societies — new forms of digital communication therefore merely reflect the postmodern condition.
- Postmodern societies are underpinned by globalisation — media transnationals have used digital communications technology such as the internet and satellite television to remove the distinction between the global and the local and to increase consumer choice in the range of knowledge and entertainment available for consumption.
- The diversity of digital forms of communication has undermined explanations that claimed absolute truths (for example, world views provided by mainstream religions, science, political movements and so on). It has resulted in the fragmentation of knowledge and encouraged people to see that there are multiple interpretations or truths — all of which have some relative value.
- People are no longer content to inherit fixed identities imposed from without, such as social class or gender identity. Instead social media networks and virtual communities offer people a plurality of identities from which to choose and consume and so subvert traditional forms of identity.
- Audiences are immersed in so much information in the digital postmodern age that they find it difficult to distinguish between real life and the digital version of reality, which Baudrillard calls **'hyper-reality'**. This has led to some concerns about how people use digital forms of communication and whether such forms of communication are healthy for identity and relationships.

**Hybridised global identity** Refers to the idea that in an increasingly hybridised world a person's beliefs or behaviour may be influenced by a mixture of the local and the global, and the traditional and the modern. For example, people who use global and modern social networking sites such as Facebook may continue to subscribe to traditional beliefs and local customs, although some of the latter may be modified by their social media experience.

**Hyper-reality** Refers to the simulation or copy of reality such as that found in places like Disneyland or in films. Some postmodernists argue that people find it increasingly difficult to distinguish between reality and hyper-reality.

However, postmodern ideas about digital communication can be criticised because they often fail to recognise inequalities in access to such technology. Consequently, postmodernism fails to offer any explanation for why some groups experience a digital divide and 'muted voice' despite the diversity of choice available in digital forms of communication. Postmodernists probably exaggerate the impact of the 'digital information explosion' on ordinary people's capacity to bring about change in their social identities and lives.

**Digital divide** Refers to inequalities in access to and use of digital technologies. For example, some people cannot afford to invest in smartphones.

## Summary

- There is no universal agreement on how to define globalisation, whether it is actually occurring or, if it is, what its causes are.
- It is accepted that the rapid advances in digital technology in the past 20 years have compressed distance in space and time. Instantaneous communication with any part of the world at any time has had the effect of making the world seem a smaller place.
- Marxists generally see global processes such as digital social networks as ideological because ownership of digital media is concentrated in the hands of a small number of media corporations.
- Marxists argue that digital social networks are generally geared to reproducing and legitimating capitalism although Castells believes that a networked global society can produce a new type of popular politics that can bring about real social change.
- Feminists see the internet and digital communication as a positive weapon against misogyny and patriarchy.
- Postmodernists see the globalisation of digital communications as positive because they argue it will produce more cultural diversity as hybrid cultures emerge.

# What is the impact of digital forms of communication in a global context?

## The impact of digital forms of communication

### Social inequalities

Some sociologists are concerned about what has been described as a digital divide, that is, inequalities are apparent in terms of who has access to digital forms of communication, particularly computers, broadband and internet access, and smartphones. In particular, access to and use of digital communication and being regularly and positively connected to others in networks bring about social capital. Conversely some groups may be denied access to such social capital.

### The generational divide

The quick-moving nature of the digital world means that younger users come of age in a vastly different media environment than those who were born just a few years apart and this makes it difficult to ascertain whether there is a generational divide in the use of digital communications. When digital technology first took off in the 1990s, it was probably true that the older generation, that is, the 50+ age group, was left behind by a so-called '**net generation**'. However, in the twenty-first century, micro-generation gaps are now apparent, with each group of children uniquely influenced by the latest digital tools available in their formative stages of development.

Prensky refers to these young people as '**digital natives**' because the internet is a 'natural' environment into which they are fully integrated. Fluency in digital culture is second nature to them and they feel a strong sense of community when online. Most of them are confident users of multiple devices on which they multitask.

Research suggests that those in the **net generation** who are now in their mid-30s and early-40s still spend time talking on their smartphones, still watch television and use e-mail frequently. However, the micro-generation of the early to mid-2000s — the so-called **iGeneration** — spends considerably more time texting than talking on the phone, tends to communicate more over instant-messenger networks and are more likely to be involved in active and regular engagement with the internet, for example uploading, blogging and networking. It may be the case that the next micro-generation of digital communication users will be very different from their older siblings because the technology is evolving so swiftly.

The 2015 Ofcom survey suggests that the macro-generational divides between young and middle-aged or elderly users may now be in decline as older age groups (digital immigrants) increasingly engage in online activities such as social networking via smartphones and tablets.

### The digital class divide

Some sociologists such as Helsper have argued that digital communications are dominated by middle-class usage because this social class can afford to invest in the most recent digital technology. In contrast, it is argued that the revolution in digital

**Social capital** Refers to the emotional, psychological, social and economic benefits that derive from being a member of a group or digital network.

**Exam tip**

Pick up marks for interpretation skills by giving examples of social capital for groups such as young people or the elderly.

**Digital natives** Refers to people who have used digital communications since their early childhood and consequently are naturally skilled in the use of digital devices and software.

**Net generation** Refers to the first generation of internet users in the 1990s.

**iGeneration** Refers to those born after 2000.

**Knowledge check 10**

What is the difference between the net generation and the iGeneration?

communications has created a **digital underclass** because the poor lack the resources to join in with this new media usage. Helsper claims that this digital underclass is characterised by unemployment, lower education levels and low digital skills.

Evidence suggests that although the digital class divide has narrowed in recent years, it still exists. For example, surveys demonstrate that the so-called digital underclass has increased its use of the internet at a much slower rate than other social groups and those members of this group that do have internet access rate their skills as poorer than other more educated groups. The 2015 Ofcom survey also found that 95% of the AB socioeconomic group use a range of new media devices to go online in any location compared with only 75% of the DE socioeconomic group and 86% of all socioeconomic groups. Three-quarters of ABs own a smartphone compared to only 54% of DEs.

### A gendered digital divide

Li and Kirkup (2007) found significant gender differences between men and women in the UK in their use of digital communication. Men were more likely than women to use e-mail or chat rooms, and men played more computer games on consoles such as the X-Box than women. Ofcom (2015) reported that in 2014 adult males in the UK accessed the internet for an average of 23.3 hours per week compared with 17.8 hours for adult females. Women (67%) were slightly more likely than men (60%) to go online and to use social media sites.

### The global divide

According to the World Bank, in 2012, about three-quarters of the world's population had access to a mobile phone. There are now 6 billion mobile subscriptions in use worldwide, of which nearly 5 billion are in developing countries. However, the West still has greater access to mobile broadband and the internet than the less developed world.

Mobile phone use has spread particularly quickly in Africa. In 2014, it was estimated that 72% of Africans use mobile phones. However, there are regional disparities in access to mobile phones — for example, in Eritrea, only 5% of the population owns a mobile phone while over 70% of people in South Africa, Nigeria and Kenya have such phones.

Smartphones (those that can access the internet and applications) are less widely used. Only 18% of Africans had access to a smartphone in 2014 although significant minorities own these devices in several nations, including 34% of South Africans and 27% of Nigerians (compared with 64% of Americans).

Furthermore, only 7% of Africa's inhabitants are online. This is because mobile connectivity in Africa is limited. Again, digital connectivity is highest in South Africa and Nigeria. Difficulties of access to the internet are also compounded by the fact that most of the language of the world wide web is English and the fact that a fairly large proportion of people in African countries are illiterate.

### People's identity

Social networking platforms such as Facebook have become the most important infrastructure through which people organise their lives and interact with others in the twenty-first century. In particular, Facebook has become the major agency for

**Digital underclass**
Refers to those who cannot afford or do not have the skills to use digital forms of communication.

**Knowledge check 11**

Identify three reasons why a digital divide exists in Africa.

packaging, promoting and presenting the self for public consumption. People use Facebook (and other social media platforms like Twitter, Snapchat and Instagram) to project their identity out into the world; to show who they are. Virtual-world sites such as Second Life enable people to choose alternative identities. All in all, then, new forms of digital communication have given people greater choice in selecting and constructing the identity that they want to present to the wider world.

Van Dijk argues that people have a vested interest in what Castells calls 'mass self-communication' because they subscribe to the view that disclosing information about their identity is closely associated with popularity. Identity is therefore a social product constructed by members of social networks for consumption by others in return for admiration and social approval. According to Turkle, internet-based social networks free people of the burdens of their physical identities and allow them to present 'better' versions of themselves.

An interesting dimension of digital media is the fact that millions of people like to construct new identities for themselves in online virtual worlds. Boellstorff has conducted research into Second Life, which is the most popular of these worlds, and found that the experience of virtual worlds can reshape ideas about people's identity. For example, both men and women users of Second Life may experiment with identity by adopting avatars of the opposite sex to their real-life selves or by adopting gender-neutral cyborg identities. Similarly, Carter's research on another virtual community, CyberCity, observes that users see their online identities as just as important as their offline identities, and that friendships made online often migrate into the real world.

## Youth and identity

Gardner and Davis observe that young people are the most frequent users of social media. Van Dijk claims social networking sites have replaced e-mail and the phone as the preferred mode of interaction for teenagers. Gardner and Davis's research indicates that young people take a great deal of care in how they present themselves online for public consumption. They identify three trends in this **presentation of self**:

1  Many young people construct a socially desirable and polished self online. This 'glammed-up' online identity generally exaggerates the more socially attractive aspects of the person's personality but downplays less 'cool' traits. This generally means that a young person's online identity may be more outgoing and extroverted than their offline everyday identity.

2  Some young people adopt a range of fictitious identities because they want to represent themselves in different ways on different sites. They are responding to different audiences who may have different expectations. For example, a person may construct a Facebook identity to attract maximum connectedness, a Twitter identity which is 'edgy' in its commentary on events, an avatar identity in Second Life which has characteristics that the user lacks in real life and a Reddit identity which is deliberately intended to provoke other people.

3  Once the self has been constructed on a social networking platform like Facebook, there is evidence that young people then engage in **identity performance** in that free time is mainly taken up checking phones in

**Mass self-communication**
Refers to use of social networking sites like Facebook to communicate information about ourselves to hundreds or thousands of people.

**Knowledge check 12**

Identify two research findings with regard to identity that research by Boellstorff and Carter discovered.

**Presentation of self**
Refers to the public persona that we project to the world via social networking sites. We may, for example, exaggerate aspects of our real selves and be partial in what we tell the world about ourselves.

**Identity performance**
Refers to the ways we attempt to manage and control other people's impressions of us.

order to manage the online impressions others have of them by 'liking' what others upload as well as updating their own profile and status.

Some observers have suggested that young people's obsession with their digital or virtual identity has created a number of modern-day problems.

- Gardner and Davis argue that this constant self-projection and self-tracking online reduces the time teenagers have for self-contemplation and real-life interaction with others. They observe that the maintenance of virtual identity means that teenagers are more **narcissistic** compared with previous generations.
- Twenge argues that fear of negative reaction to their identity performance is producing rising levels of moodiness, anxiety, sadness and isolation among teenagers.
- Turkle suggests that young people are mentally 'tethered' to their digital devices, as symbolised by their need to constantly track and check their connections. She argues that this has weakened young people's ability to develop an autonomous sense of self. They are too dependent on how other people react to them online. She claims that it is as if their thoughts and feelings are not real until they have been validated by others online.

### The elderly and identity

There are signs that the greater take-up of digital communication by older people may have benefits for their self-esteem and identity. Researchers who carried out a study of elderly people's use of social media in Britain and Italy found that training older vulnerable people to use social media improves their cognitive capacity, increases a sense of self-competence and could have a beneficial overall impact on their mental health and physical well-being. Researchers found that the majority of their sample who had the hardware and the know-how reported feeling less isolated because of the digital connections they could make with relatives, friends and people with shared interests.

### Disability and identity

Ginsburg argues that interactive digital technologies provide powerful platforms for people with disabilities because they enable them to engage in first-person discussion of their worlds and experiences. There are three broad ways in which disabled people have used digital media to establish online identity:

1 Digital video activism — there has been an explosion of YouTube blogs featuring people with a range of disabilities encompassing autism to wheelchair use. The net sum of this has been to create a community in which those who have difficulty in face-to-face conversation and those who may be restricted to a particular identity can speak to an audience about their experience of disability.

2 Miller observes that Facebook has been used by people with disabilities to create support networks such as Disability Rights UK, Dancing Giraffe and Ableize, which aim to provide the 50,000 diverse disabled people in the UK with a voice and political influence by connecting them to each other online.

**Knowledge check 13**

In what ways do young people present themselves on social networking sites?

**Narcissism** Refers to excessive love or admiration of ourselves.

**Exam tip**

Note that most of the benefits identified in this section are examples of social capital.

3  Many people with disabilities use virtual-world sites such as Second Life or Virtual Ability. Boellstorff observes that Second Life enables disabled people to take control of identity and their interactions with others by adopting virtual identities that are denied to them in real life. For example, people dependent on wheelchairs in real life can adopt avatars which walk, run and dance, while text chat equalises deaf people's ability to talk to everyone compared with the real world in which only a minority of non-disabled people are familiar with sign language. Virtual Ability has been designed by people with disabilities as a virtual community of support. It provides opportunities for disabled people to virtually experience a range of activities that they are excluded from in the real world, such as dancing, mountain climbing, trampolining and skydiving, in order to improve confidence, self-esteem and social skills.

However, although participation in the digital world by disabled people has considerably increased, the design of most digital media can also be disabling. For example, small fonts can be a problem for the visually impaired, while typing may not be possible for others.

## Relationships

Digital social media in all its forms facilitate human interaction and relationships by constructing a **participatory culture**. Turkle (2011) refers to new-media users as 'cyborgs' because they are always connected to one other, regardless of where they are, via their laptops, tablets and smartphones. Gardner and Davis also observe that internet-enabled digital devices have enabled relationships because they transcend geographical and temporal barriers. They allow for immediacy of communication with others.

Young people, in particular, have taken advantage of digital technology to engage in frequent on-the-run communication with friends. In the UK over 90% of 16–24 year-olds send at least one text per day, while 73% also use social networking sites to send messages and maintain relationships. The average UK person sends 50 texts per week although this is small compared to the 'typical' teen, who sends up to 60 texts per day. Gardner and Davis suggest that young people now 'hang out' at Facebook (as they once did in physical places like cafes or McDonalds).

Several advantages of online relationships have been identified by Van Dijk as well as Gardner and Davis. Accumulating connections or online relationships is empowering and enriching because it produces social capital. Social capital broadly refers to the resources accumulated through relationships among people. This means that it has collective value for all concerned because connections and the opportunities which result from them are shared and reciprocated. For example:

- Membership of an online community may provide opportunities for people with similar interests to find and interact with one another. This type of capital is known as 'bonding social capital' and produces shared information flows that

**Participatory culture**
A culture in which we are invited to connect to each other because we share the same interests or we wish to acquire various types of social capital or supports.

may throw up opportunities for jobs or mutual aid. For example, belonging to a Facebook community of A-level sociology students may bring benefits in terms of shared information about how to pass the exam.

■ Membership of a particular online community may lead to relationships being established with others who are very different. This is known as 'bridging social capital'. For example, feminists may wish to bond with other feminists but social networking sites such as Twitter may lead to feminists realising that seemingly different political causes focused on aspects of inequality may in fact have a great deal in common with their cause. This may lead to political alliances which increase the potential for social change.

■ Online texting and Facebooking function to micro-coordinate activity among friends. Gardner and Davis suggest digital communication is used as a 'virtual tap on the shoulder', establishing and maintaining links between friends who are physically separated. Cummings found that e-mail, instant messaging and social networking sites helped students stay in frequent contact with friends and family when separated by geography. Miller observes that, thanks to Facebook, people can maintain friendships over distance with less expenditure of time or money. He argues that use of social media extends existing relationships which may be weak because of distance or because they have lapsed over time and develops them into more meaningful relationships.

■ Texting and social networking may function simply to fill time and alleviate boredom.

■ Sites like Facebook may be a social lifeline, particularly for isolated, shy or disabled individuals, to stay connected to other people. Bargh and McKenna found that social platforms can help those with low self-esteem relate to others because they lower barriers to interaction (for example, it is not face-to-face) and this may make it easier for some people to disclose their feelings to others. Similarly, Gardner and Davis suggest texting and instant messaging is more private, intimate and less risky for sharing information about oneself.

■ Social media enable minority groups that have traditionally been denied a voice in the traditional media — known as 'muted voices' — such as those with disabilities or ethnic minorities or tribal groups to create supportive communities that can highlight their everyday experience and coordinate activism.

■ Online relationships may compensate for the fact that youth today have limited geographical freedom, enjoy less free time and are subject to more parental rules.

■ Social media can positively change how people work. For example, thousands of people including this author use digital technology to work from home. This practice may benefit family life.

■ Boyd argues that young people's involvement in public digital networks helps them to manage the transition from adolescence to adult society and assists their understanding of how to successfully negotiate public life. This is possible because sites like Facebook mirror and magnify both the positive and negative aspects of public everyday life.

**Knowledge check 14**

Identify three types of social capital that derive from relationships on social networking sites such as Facebook.

## Criticisms of social networks

Critics of social networks suggest that the costs of this online revolution may outweigh the benefits. It is argued that digital forms of communication are actually bad for relationships for the following reasons:

1   Marxists such as Fuchs argue that it is the powerful who control digital communication and social media, and this undermines the concept of a participatory digital culture. Fuchs argues that as a result connectedness is less important than connectivity. Van Dijk illustrates this when he observes that the **algorithms** developed by social networking sites like Facebook for commercial reasons increasingly determine what people like, want, know or find. The aim of these algorithms is not to connect people but to keep them online as long as possible and to maximise the possibility that they will click on and connect to other commercial sites. Fuchs argues that friendship and connectedness have become commodified. Social media activity is not as voluntary as people believe it to be. Algorithms shepherd people towards making 'choices' that benefit capitalist agencies such as advertisers. Social media content may therefore simply reflect capitalist ideology.

2   There are concerns about how the data collected by sites such as Facebook might be used. Facebook has already been accused of violating the privacy of its users. Other sites have used cookies to keep their users under surveillance.

   There is also evidence that criminals are targeting social media and/ or using digital media to commit cybercrimes such as **identity theft**. It is becoming apparent to politicians and law-makers that new forms of social media (as well as their content) are very difficult to police.

3   The quality of online relationships or 'friends' has been questioned. Turkle observes that people boast about how many people they have 'friended' on Facebook, but research on the nature of friendship in the USA concludes that Americans say they have few real friends. Miller observes that critics of Facebook suggest that 'friending' represents a 'kind of inflation' of superficial and weak relationships that diminishes the value of true friendship. It is argued that the quality of Facebook relationships can feel inauthentic because they lack the intimacy, vulnerability and physical closeness that characterise real relationships. Gardner and Davis argue that 'friends' may be connected but they may not always be connecting.

4   It is suggested that social networking sites may cause alienation and loneliness because they create the impression that other people have more friends and are therefore having more fun. Moreover, looking at other people's achievements may make young people feel inadequate and even encourage them to 'stage' happiness and success. Kross and Verduyn found that frequent use of Facebook leads to people becoming less satisfied with life.

5   Digital technology can diminish the quality of face-to-face interaction if people are always focused on their phone and constantly checking for texts and social network updates. Turkle points out that although digital

> **Algorithm** A list of digital rules that computers follow in order to identify connections between things. If you buy a book from Amazon, an algorithm works out what other books you may like and recommends them to you.

> **Identity theft** Occurs when criminals access their victims' personal information and then use it for their own gain.

**Knowledge check 15**

What does the phrase 'friends may be connected but they may not always be connecting' mean?

forms of communication connect users to more people, this has also resulted in greater anxiety. She notes devotion to checking the mobile phone is almost religious. When mobile phones are misplaced, anxiety levels rise. People feel cut off from reality. Turkle argues that this is unhealthy behaviour.

6  Digital technology is disruptive because it may reduce family time and closeness. Turkle has argued that the proto-communities of social networking sites and online fantasy gaming such as Second Life are increasingly replacing real communities composed of family, extended kin and neighbours. As a result, the 'post-familial' family in which family members spend more time interacting with their gadgets than with each other is becoming the norm. Livingstone (2009) in a similar analysis argues that children today communicate more with the virtual outside world than with adult members of their own family. Parents often have to text or Facebook their children to gain their attention at meal times.

7  It is argued that digital media have had a coarsening effect on young people. In particular, it is suggested that they have had the effect of making young people less empathetic and therefore 'meaner' online than they are in person. Online bullying, sexting, grooming and sexual harassment are now recognised as problems of the digital age. Other studies have documented the emotional effects of easy online access to pornography and have expressed fears that adolescent boys' attitudes towards sexual relationships are consequently being shaped by deviant and unrepresentative sexual role models. All of these issues are difficult for sociologists to investigate and for the authorities to police.

8  Despite greater connectivity, some groups are still unable to access or participate in social media.

## The impact of digital forms of communication on culture

### Conflict and change

Castells argues that in the digital age many people have moved away from expressing their political and social concerns through hierarchical and bureaucratic organisations such as governments, political parties, pressure groups, trade unions, religions and so on. The easy availability of digital forms of communication now means that people can organise themselves into non-hierarchical and non-bureaucratic digital networks of like-minded individuals who can mutually share information on the web and organise collective action.

Castells argues that this **civil society** approach is now an alternative source of political power that is challenging the power of both the state and the market. For example, successful petitioning of those in power has been carried out through Facebook, Twitter and sites such as Change.org. Itzoe observes that the internet and social media have been extensively used by the anti-globalisation movement (also known as the global justice movement) to successfully organise large worldwide protests against global organisations such as the World Trade Organization and the International Monetary Fund, which are seen as partly responsible for global inequality and

**Post-familial** The post-familial family is a family that interacts and communicates via social media and other digital devices rather than face-to-face.

**Exam tip**

Don't forget to include the concept of cultural homogenisation when you discuss the impact of digital forms of communication on culture.

**Civil society** Refers to the community of ordinary citizens who are linked by common interests and collective actions. It is argued that civil society is increasingly challenging traditional sources of power such as states and corporations.

injustice. Murthy claims that Twitter has the potential to shape many aspects of people's social, political and economic lives. For example, it has proved extremely useful in terms of communicating information about social protest movements such as the Occupy protests in London and New York in 2011, while websites such as WikiLeaks have challenged the power of both the state and large corporations by publishing leaked documents alleging government and corporate misconduct. Digital activists such as the hacker group Anonymous have also engaged in cyberattacks on government and corporate websites.

There is also evidence that global communication systems and social networks can assist local cultures to rid themselves of repressive political systems such as dictatorships. Both Castells and Kassim argue that the so-called Arab Spring movement that occurred between 2010 and 2013 succeeded in removing totalitarian dictators in Tunisia and Egypt because of global social networks. For example, Facebook was used in Egypt to schedule public protests, Twitter to coordinate, and YouTube to show the world how the authorities had reacted. Kassim argues that these global networks helped Arab people in Egypt and Tunisia to overcome their fears and to take to the streets.

However, critics argue that the role of social media in the Arab Spring has been grossly exaggerated. Curran argues that the Arab Spring was caused by deep-seated economic, political and religious factors, while Wilson and Dunn found that face-to-face interaction, television and print media were more important than social media in getting people onto the streets. Curran concludes that social media played a role in the build-up of dissent and the coordination of protests but they did not cause the uprisings — they merely facilitated them (along with other forms of traditional media).

Moreover, ideas about the ability of digital communication networks to construct an alternative civil society that can bring about real social change are undermined by the global divide in access to and participation in digital networks. For example, in 2015 the UN announced that 4 billion people — 57% of the world's population and 90% of those who live in the 48 poorest countries — have no access to the internet.

Furthermore, critics argue that it is a fact that states and digital corporations continue to exercise much greater power than digitalised civil society groups. There is a growing tendency in the digital corporate world for power to be concentrated in fewer and fewer more powerful hands. Martell argues that digital technology therefore gives a false impression of more power being given to a greater number of people. He suggests that digital technology may be only a quantitative rather than a qualitative improvement since political information could be obtained before the internet, albeit more awkwardly and slowly. Martell concludes that technologically the internet is revolutionary but it does not necessarily follow that it will have a revolutionary impact on cultural or political life.

Keen is also critical of the idea that the internet and digital technology have the power to politically change the world. He argues that the internet is too chaotically organised to be effective in bringing about change. Moreover, he argues that social networking sites such as Facebook and blogging do not contribute to the democratic process in any way because they are merely vehicles for shameless self-promotion. He further argues that the content of Twitter and blogs often goes unchecked and, consequently, uninformed opinion, lies

**Knowledge check 16**

Identify one argument for and one argument against the idea that digital technology played a big role in the Arab Spring.

and trolling are the norm, rather than considered political analysis and expertise. Hader too argues that the power of Twitter to change the world is grossly exaggerated when he described Twitter users as ineffectual and pseudo laptop and iPad revolutionaries.

## Cultural defence

There are a number of ways in which societies and cultures have attempted to protect their domestic media and cultural industries:

- Some countries, for example France, protect their domestic media and cultural industries against the cultural homogenisation brought about by globalisation.
- Some countries have taken control of their digital media. For example, China has blocked all references to the word 'democracy' on its most popular search engine and denies its citizens access to websites such as Wikipedia. All internet use is closely monitored by the authorities. This censorship and surveillance is referred to as the 'great firewall of China'.
- The Muslim world has developed internet websites, political blogs and satellite television channels such as Al-Jazeera to provide an alternative interpretation of what is going on in the Arab world and elsewhere, thereby resisting and opposing Western interpretations.
- In Africa, the expansion of mobile phone technology has had a number of positive effects for local cultures and economies. Greater access to smartphones and social networks has empowered young people to organise themselves online and demand better leadership of their societies. Moreover, there is evidence that mobile phones have had a significant effect on African economies by connecting young consumers over vast distances. Culture too has been enhanced by digital technology. Literacy rates are improving because young people have access to e-books and digital libraries. Healthcare has been improved because it is now possible to access internet medical service providers.
- There is evidence that social networking sites such as Facebook are being used by migrant populations to facilitate connections with their homeland. These connections help them to preserve and defend aspects of their culture, especially language, customs, traditions and religious rites. McKay found when examining the digital experience of Filipinos living and working in London that they used social networking sites to insulate themselves from the individualism that they claimed dominated Western culture. Social networking with relatives and friends in the Philippines meant they could digitally return to the comfort of the types of cultural relationships that they had physically left behind — relationships characterised by obligations to the extended family and ancestors, involvement in the local community from which they had originated, and religious traditions.
- Culturalsurvival.org documents the diverse range of ways in which indigenous tribes and isolated communities are starting to use digital technology to gain a voice that can help defend their cultures from exploitation by corporate interests and other threats.

**Cultural defence** Refers to the ways societies attempt to protect their local cultures from globalised culture and the way digital forms of communication are used to support and enhance local culture.

■ However, ISIS is also utilising social media in a very sophisticated fashion — to defend and disseminate its version of Islam. Since 2014 ISIS has posted (mainly on Twitter) photos and statements to highlight details of its operations, including the number of bombings, suicide missions, beheadings and assassinations it has carried out. The group also produces professional promotional videos and urges support for its 'one billion campaign', which calls on Muslims to post messages, photos and videos on Twitter, Instagram and YouTube in support of ISIS. In April 2014, the group even developed a free internet application called The Dawn of Glad Tidings, which automatically posts tweets — approved by ISIS media managers — to the accounts of the application's subscribed users.

## Glocalisation

Martell observes that glocalisation has two elements to it. First, Western media and cultural producers often adapt their products so that they appeal to local markets and audiences. For example, MTV adapts its programming according to the cultural likes and dislikes of particular countries such as Japan, India, Mexico, Spain, France and so on and mixes Western music with that produced locally.

Second, local cultures select and appropriate elements of Westernised global culture that please them and which they modify and adapt to local culture and needs. In other words, they 'localise the global' to produce a hybridised popular culture. A good example of this is the Indian film industry — Bollywood combines contemporary Western ideas about entertainment with traditional Hindu myth, history and culture.

Another good example is Facebook. Miller argues that there is no such thing as Facebook from the perspective of cultural relativity. Facebook is only the aggregate of its regional usage; for example, Facebook in Trinidad is not Facebook in London because two very different cultures, Trinidadian and British, use Facebook in very different ways which reflect their cultural priorities. Miller's research on Facebook use in Trinidad found that it reflects aspects of Trinidadian culture. He observes that locals refer to it as 'Fasbook' or 'Macobook'. These terms are not accidental — they deliberately mirror the cultural inclinations of Trinidadian society, especially the characteristics 'to be fas' (to try and get to know another person rather too quickly) and 'maco' (to be nosy and wanting to constantly pry into other people's business). So activity on Fasbook in Trinidad is mainly geared to getting to know somebody of the opposite sex but once people become friends with one another, they constantly meddle in one another's lives. Fasbook, then, is a good example of glocalisation because it has taken the Western idea of a digital communications network but Trinidadians' use of it reflects their local culture.

Held argues that this flow of digital culture is not just one way. Western culture has also been enriched by inputs from the popular culture of other societies. For example, many Western musicians such as Damon Albarn and Robert Plant have worked with African and Arab musicians to fuse genres of music into new forms. Some world music fuses and mixes Western dance beats with traditional styles from North Africa and Asia.

**Knowledge check 17**

Why is Bollywood a good example of a hybridised global culture?

**Glocalisation** Refers to how local cultural products are combined or fused with globalised cultural products to produce unique cultural forms or hybrids. It can also refer to how local cultures adapt and use global social networks in ways that reflect the cultural priorities and eccentricities of a particular society.

## Summary

- Not everybody enjoys equal access to digital forms of communication. Research indicates that a digital divide exists with regard to access to the internet. A digital underclass exists which is denied a digital voice.
- People use social networking sites such as Facebook and virtual worlds to package, promote and present their identities for public consumption, although some sociologists argue that young people's use of digital communication has created a set of modern-day problems for them.
- There is a debate about whether social networking sites are good for society and individuals. Some sociologists argue that they facilitate human interaction, relationships and social capital by constructing a participatory culture. Others have expressed concern that these sites have created a culture of alienation and loneliness which has diminished the quality of human relationships.
- Digital media can act as a resource that helps bring about social change. They have also been used to defend and enhance existing cultural practices.

# ■ Section B Education

## What is the role of education in society?

Sociologists have contrasting views about the role and purpose of education and also about its effects. There are Structural theories such as those of functionalists, Marxists and feminists, some of which see the very structure of society as controlling all of its institutions such as education. Some view education as having a positive function (functionalists), while others believe it serves the interests of the ruling classes (Marxists). Other theorists such as liberals, New Right and social democrats also discuss the role education can play if influenced correctly by policy and the state.

### Functionalist views on the role of education

Overall, functionalists take a positive view on the role of education. They believe above all that the education system is an important part of society, which not only prepares the individual for the world of work but also functions for the good of the economy by allocating people to jobs which make the most effective use of their talents and abilities.

Durkheim believed that education serves to create 'value consensus' and 'social solidarity', because school makes students feel as though they are part of something bigger than themselves. He suggested that students are taught subjects like history through the formal curriculum, but also the fundamental values of the society (such as meritocracy) through the hidden curriculum, which gives students a shared sense of identity and values. Students come to accept these values, therefore creating a value consensus. This gives a sense of collective belonging and students invest in this as they feel a sense of social solidarity, belonging and togetherness. These values are reinforced in school as it acts as a miniature version of society, making students work and cooperate in a formal environment with people other than family while adhering to these values. Subscribing to this value consensus gets students ready for dealing with people at work in later life.

Durkheim also believed that education is vital for teaching students the specialist skills for work. He called this a 'specialised division of labour'. Advanced industrial society is complex and requires a huge number of different skills in order to function effectively. Everyone learns the same things through the National Curriculum; however, as students progress through education, they begin to study fewer subjects and specialise more. For example, they do fewer subjects at GCSE than in the first part of secondary school, then they reduce these further at A-level, and so on, eventually meaning that they have the specialised skills and knowledge required for the economy.

Parsons suggested that school takes over as the main agent of socialisation after the family, acting as a bridge between the family and society, and that the role of education is to prepare young people for the adult world. Within the family, a child is judged by particularistic standards, meaning that they are judged as an individual in the context of their family unit, and all of their little quirks, moods and behaviours are accepted and tolerated. But these sorts of things may not be accepted so readily by wider society, so school teaches young people how to act in accordance with universal standards (e.g. you must just sit there in assembly as it is not acceptable to get up and

**Exam tip**

Make sure you have a detailed knowledge of the key theories and know a range of sociologists who are linked to each of them. Top AO1 marks are awarded for 'range and depth'.

**Value consensus** refers to the agreement of a common set of values in society (functionalism).

**Specialised division of labour** refers to a range of tasks within a social system, with each person having a specialised role. This occurs in advanced industrialised societies.

**Particularistic standards** or **universalistic standards** refers to how children are judged according to *particular* standards in the family, and standards that are the norm and specific to them, whereas in school and wider society they are judged according to *universal* standards, which are more applicable to society as a whole.

walk out even if you are bored, whereas at home you can leave a room if you choose). This is because individuals are born with the ascribed status of a child within the family and must learn how to move towards the achieved status of an adult within society — and this transition between the two is facilitated by education.

Davis and Moore believe the role of education is to make sure that the best people are placed in the best jobs in order for society to function effectively, which they call 'role allocation'. This is able to happen successfully because schools operate on meritocratic principles, meaning that if students work hard at school and are good at a subject, then they do well and can continue this in higher education. This makes sure that the best students, who are determined and talented, go on to get the best jobs in society. In this way it helps allocate roles effectively. Because we live in a stratified society and have a value consensus that this hierarchy works, we accept that those in the most important jobs get — and deserve — the best pay. Therefore this encourages students to work hard at school in order to achieve exam success and go on to get the best jobs. For example, a student who was not excellent at chemistry would not pass an A-level in the subject, therefore could not do a degree in it nor become a doctor, whereas those who were truly talented scientists and willing to work hard would be able to pursue such a career.

Critics would question whether there is really an agreed hierarchy of skills and whether people really get paid accordingly. For example, can a footballer really justifiably be paid hundreds of thousands of pounds, while a nurse or soldier is paid significantly less?

Also, other sociologists such as Marxists and feminists would disagree with this, as there are obvious differences in educational achievement, for example between different social classes, ethnic groups and genders. If education were truly meritocratic as functionalists suggest, then surely this would not occur.

## Marxist views on the role of education

Marxists take a more pessimistic view than functionalists on the role of education. They argue that, while education does prepare young people for work, this does not benefit the student or society; it actually sets them up to be exploited and alienated and preserves the position of the ruling class.

Marxists state that the education system serves the interests of capitalism. They argue that there are two main groups in society — the *ruling class* (bourgeoisie) and the *working class* (proletariat) — and they see education as negative as it transmits the ruling-class ideology and produces an obedient workforce that fits the needs of capitalism. Althusser argues that the role of education is to reproduce and legitimise ruling-class ideology. He suggests that the values of meritocracy transmitted in schools are a 'myth', and that actually the working classes are disadvantaged in the education system and conditioned to believe in a system that disadvantages them. This is all in an attempt to get young people to accept capitalism. Althusser claims that this is achieved through socialisation by the Ideological State Apparatuses. These are the different institutions in society, education being a main one. He

**Meritocracy** refers to the idea that effort + ability = rewards.

**Knowledge check 18**

What are the three key roles of education according to functionalists?

**Capitalism** refers to an economic system based on the production of goods for profit.

The **Ideological State Apparatuses** are institutions (such as the media and education) that implicitly or explicitly teach and maintain a ruling-class ideology.

suggests that school legitimises inequalities in society by teaching that grading and selecting people is just a part of life that students must accept and that unfairness comes with this, therefore justifying all the inequalities in society.

Bowles and Gintis extend this idea, agreeing that the role of education is social reproduction, but also stating that education prepares young people directly for work. They call this the 'correspondence principle' — the idea that school trains young people to be obedient proletariat when they begin their working lives. Bowles and Gintis argue the hidden and formal curriculum actually encourage obedience, boredom and disengagement from learning. The hierarchy of teachers, staff and students and the systems in school create an acceptance of authority, a sense of detachment from learning and also adherence to a set of strict rules and values that set students up for the workplace. Schools also teach the value of rewards and hard work, and Bowles and Gintis refer to this as the 'myth of meritocracy', suggesting that young people are socialised into accepting this, when in reality meritocracy does not exist and the system is just set up to preserve the position of the ruling class.

It must be questioned, however, whether the hidden curriculum is really that important. There is a standard National Curriculum that teaches standard subjects; are students really that influenced by implicit values?

Marxists are critical of functionalists as they believe that meritocracy does not exist because the working class are deliberately disadvantaged in order to preserve capitalism. But policies such as EMA, Sure Start and EAZ have sought to redress material, cultural and social barriers to education. Marxist theory depends on a structuralist view of education as a state apparatus, but in reality there is much power devolved to local education authorities (LEAs).

## Other views on the role of education

There are of course other theoretical views on the role of education, which share similarities and differences. For example, **liberal** thinker Illich would agree with Marxists that education is a means of control, but would disagree on its purpose. Illich argues that education should be a mechanism to help people grow as individuals. He proposed the 'deschooling' of society, by which he meant that formal education should be abolished and replaced by informal learning networks in which children would be encouraged to learn only about those things that interested them rather than those things set out in a school curriculum. This idea was actually put into practice at Summerhill School in Suffolk, a fee-paying school where pupils rather than teachers choose what they study.

Some sociologists may argue, however, that liberal ideas about the role of education are being addressed, with more free schools opening and a shift towards vocational education in order to meet the needs of the economy and prepare young people for work.

**Feminists** agree with Marxists and functionalists that the role of education is to socialise young people into a common set of norms and values; they argue, however, that these norms and values are patriarchal and so their role is to prepare girls for the

The **correspondence principle** is the idea that school prepares students for work as it directly mirrors how things will be when they start work.

The **hidden and formal curriculum** are the things students learn at school, both informally (hidden) through rules and expectations and formally through the timetable.

**Knowledge check 19**

What are the three key roles of education according to Marxists?

**Patriarchal** refers to the idea that society is male-dominated.

gender inequalities in society. Spender argues that the curriculum is focused on males and that teachers are more encouraging of boys. She believes it is fundamentally what is learned in school that shapes the outcomes of girls:

> What is considered inherently interesting is knowledge about men. Because men control the records, and the value system, it is generally believed that it is men who have done all the exciting things, it is men who have made (his)tory, made discoveries, made inventions and performed feats of skill and courage — according to men. These are the important activities and only men can engage in them, so we are led to believe. And so it is that the activities of men become the curriculum.
>
> (Dale Spender, 1982)

Also, according to Kelly, the resources used in subjects such as science are set up to be more appealing to boys, alienating girls in the classroom and creating inequality of opportunity. This creates a reproduction of inequality; girls are socialised to accept the unfairness and are additionally already disadvantaged when entering the workplace because of this.

In opposition to this, however, it could be argued that policies and campaigns such as GIST (Girls into Science and Technology, a programme run in some schools in the 1980s) and the WISE campaign (Women into Science and Engineering, launched in 1984 and still running programmes such as Discover! to encourage girls into STEM subjects) have encouraged young women into male-dominated professions such as engineering. Do these barriers really still exist as much as feminists suggest?

The **social democratic approach** is similar to the functionalist approach in that it believes there should be meritocracy in education, but the key difference is that it believes this should be achieved through policy as education is not yet meritocratic. Social democrats such as Halsey suggest that the education system has not achieved this as there is not yet equality of opportunity, evidenced by the fact that there are still differences in attainment between groups of people in society. Social democrats argue that there is a 'wastage of ability' as some children do not have the same opportunities as others, meaning that many talented students are not able to progress due to a lack of equality of opportunity. They believe that the role of education is to provide a trained and specialised workforce for a complex modern industrial society, and therefore that investment in the education system should be made in order to address this issue.

The **New Right**'s thinkers, like the social democrats, believe that education should meet the needs of the economy, but they believe this should be done by raising standards through marketisation and competition, which would then benefit the economy as it would produce the best people for jobs. This should be done through differing types of education. The fundamental belief is that the state should not control things as it prevents growth and initiative; the New Right sees the Government as currently taking too much control and creating a 'nanny state'. The New Right argues that the education system should be fragmented into different types of schools, such as free schools and specialist schools, which would create marketisation and competition and would drive up standards. Like social democrats, its thinkers are more concerned with policy impacts on education than with trying to address its actual role and purpose.

**Exam tip**

Good evaluation and tone will not just oppose an argument, but will pick out similarities as well as differences between ideas and theories.

Marketisation refers to the introduction of competition to things that were previously state-controlled.

**Knowledge check 20**

What is the key similarity between the social democratic and New Right approaches?

# Education and preparation for work

Theorists also discuss the relationship between education and work. As previously mentioned, functionalists believe that education prepares young people well for the world of work in terms of equipping them with the right values and ethics for work, but also by allowing the correct people to be placed in the correct roles.

The New Right extends these ideas as it takes a very policy-based approach to education and believes the way to achieve successful role allocation is to create the best possible opportunities within education itself. After her election in 1979, Prime Minister Margaret Thatcher implemented policies to reflect this ideology, and sought to place power within the schools themselves in order to allow them to control their own organisation and be the best they could be. Thatcher believed that up to this point there had been a 'nanny state' that controlled too many things centrally, and that power should be placed back locally within the schools themselves as they were best placed to know and understand what was needed for their area.

For example, Durkheim discusses how schools socialise pupils into a common set of values that prepare them to accept the world of work, authority and hierarchy based on meritocratic principles. Davis and Moore develop this by suggesting that school successfully allocates roles by filtering the most talented and dedicated into the correct jobs through a process of examinations.

The New Right also firmly believes in parentocracy, which means parents having the right to choose schools for their children rather than being forced to send them to the nearest local provision. The New Right argues that education needs to take a more vocational approach and to train young people in skills for the workplace rather than just focusing on academia. This was seen in the introduction of vocational education by Thatcher through programmes such as YTS (Youth Training Schemes) and NVQs. In criticism of the New Right, however, the theory focuses on raising standards and preparation for work through marketisation, but in reality choice is limited, particularly in the catchment areas of some of the best schools where property prices might be too high for many people.

Marxists, however, while agreeing with functionalists and the New Right that school prepares students for work, think that it is preparing most of them for a life of being working class. Willis' research found that some working-class lads rejected school and the idea that success meant acquiring qualifications. In contrast, they redefined success as getting manual jobs in the local car factory. They consequently formed an anti-school subculture which saw success as 'having a laff' at the expense of teachers and more academic boys. To what extent is Willis' theory still relevant? The study was carried out in the 1970s, when the economic and social landscapes were very different. Do working-class boys truthfully reject school as irrelevant or could it possibly be more down to maturity levels or other factors?

Bowles and Gintis also agree that school prepares young people for work, suggesting that the day-to-day life of being at school is similar to the workplace, calling this the 'correspondence principle'. They argue that actually it prepares children to accept the mundane nature of working life. School makes students learn to accept authority, rules and boredom, training them to be obedient and compliant workers in the future.

Some sociologists, however, such as Finn, suggest that school does not adequately prepare students for work as certain aspects of education, such as vocational training and qualifications, are actually seen by many as an inferior qualification to the more academic A-level subjects. He goes on to suggest that 'on-the-job training' and placements are low quality and poorly regulated, with some young trainees being exploited just to do menial tasks such as make tea.

**Knowledge check 21**

What is the main Marxist criticism of vocational education?

## Summary

- There are similarities between the functionalist and Marxist views as well as differences. For example, they both recognise the importance of the hidden curriculum and role allocation within education, but disagree about the purpose that these serve and who they benefit.
- The role of education for functionalists is to create value consensus and role allocation for a specialised division of labour and to act as a bridge between family and society.
- For Marxists its role is to socialise young people into a ruling-class ideology through a 'myth of meritocracy' that supports capitalism.
- Liberals believe its role is to prepare young people for work but they feel the education system does not always do this and that it should be done through alternative means.
- Feminists argue that education is patriarchal and helps prepare girls for future gender inequality.
- The New Right and social democrats also see the role of education as a means of preparation for work but are more interested in how policy impacts on this than on analysing its purpose.

# What are the patterns and trends of educational inequalities?

## Differential educational achievement

Not all groups of people achieve equally in society. The exam requires you to be aware of and understand patterns and trends in relation to these differences and also the explanations as to why these occur. It is important to note that while this section is separated into class, ethnicity and gender, the boundaries are rarely that distinct, for example there are often links between class, certain ethnic groups and gender, with some students being far more at risk of underachievement.

## Social class and educational achievement

There are clear links between social class and achievement. Children from lower-class backgrounds are less likely to achieve the same levels as middle-class children both at the age of 11 (SATs) and also at GCSE. This then limits their abilities to progress to further education. Sociologists put forward three key arguments for this: material factors, cultural factors and 'in-school' factors.

### Material factors

Material factors are financial; these can lead to lack of both resources and access to education. Working-class children are more likely to be subject to this. Smith and Noble argue that working-class children may face these '**barriers to learning**' as parents cannot afford uniforms, computers or textbooks. As a result these students do not have the resources to help them and so may find studying at home difficult or may fall behind. Students who do not have the correct uniform are easily identifiable and this can lead to stigma and bullying, making them feel marginalised and less likely to want to participate in school life. The lack of correct uniform also prevents students from benefiting from opportunities in school such as becoming prefects; such opportunities are important for personal statements and CVs, and their lack can limit progression. Diet is also linked to money and this may lead to more frequent illness and time off school, which impacts on achievement.

Gerwitz et al. are usually associated with Marxist ideas of cultural and social capital, but overall this is a good example of how these ideas can be linked to material factors. For example, middle-class parents were likely to be in possession of economic capital and therefore able to buy houses within catchment areas of good schools, but were also able to utilise their cultural and social capital to get their children into the best schools. According to Gerwitz et al., middle-class parents are 'privileged skilled choosers' and are able to research and appeal for their children to get into these schools, maximising their chances of success even if they do not happen to live in the right catchment areas. Working-class students are less likely to possess economic, social or cultural capital and are therefore likely to live in poorer areas with less well-performing schools, and their parents are less likely to be aware of how to manipulate the system.

Callender and Jackson argue that this pattern of material disadvantage also extends to higher education, suggesting that the increase in tuition fees and the replacement of grants with loans that need to be paid back have discouraged working-class students

**Exam tip**

During revision, create a spider or Venn diagram to show all the links between class, ethnicity and gender in terms of educational achievement. Which groups in society are the most deprived? How do they intersect with these three categories and how can you apply your knowledge?

from applying to university due to a 'fear of debt' or 'debt aversion'. It is possible that a lack of role models or of family who understand the process and financial implications of student loans may mean that they are less likely to apply.

Social democrats agree and acknowledge this to be an issue, so their influence over New Labour policy resulted in policies such as **New Deal** and **EMA** being introduced as a means for families who suffered material disadvantage to overcome these issues.

## Cultural factors

There are also theories to suggest that the norms, values and attitudes of different social classes favour the achievement of certain groups of children. The attitudes and practices of middle-class families set children up well for education, facilitating them to achieve, whereas those of working-class families do not.

Feinstein argues that parental interest is a key factor in attainment. This is due to various factors including material, but parental interest and the value placed on education was significantly different between social classes, with working-class parents seeing it as less important. Children were tested academically at 22 months and then their educational achievement was tracked at the age of 26. The children of educated or wealthy parents who scored poorly in the early tests had caught up, whereas the low-achieving children of poorer parents had not. Feinstein concluded this was in part because parents were less likely to be involved in their children's education if they came from a background of poverty.

Marxist Bourdieu takes a slightly different perspective and suggests it is not down to the interest of parents alone but actually the cultural environment in which the child grows up. He argues that middle-class families are in possession of **cultural capital**. This is an interest in and knowledge of the arts, current affairs and culture. As a result they are more likely to encourage play and leisure based around these, for example trips to a museum or discussion of current affairs. Since the school curriculum is also based around these things, middle-class children have an educational advantage. Bourdieu acknowledges that this is not the only factor and also talks about the combined effect of middle-class parents having economic capital to be able to afford access to culture, as these activities are costly, but states that it is the access to and immersion in these things that is key. His point illustrates how education seeks to reproduce inequalities to support and maintain capitalism, so the construction of a curriculum based around cultural capital excludes working-class students and maintains cultural reproduction.

Bernstein suggests that speech patterns emanating from the home affect educational achievement. He argues that there are two types of **speech codes**: restricted and elaborated. *Restricted* is an informal 'chatty' type of language and *elaborated* is more complex and articulate. He suggests that middle-class families are more likely to use elaborated code as well as restricted code, whereas working-class families do not. Education is taught and assessed in elaborated code, so working-class children are immediately disadvantaged when they enter education as they are used to only one type of code and are in effect grappling with a new 'language' alongside educational content, which is why they are less likely to match their middle-class peers.

It must be asked, however, to what extent we really operate in and measure culture or social class? These are very complex categories and are constantly changing.

**New Deal** refers to a 1998 initiative by Blair (New Labour) of encouraging people into work via training and volunteering.

**EMA** Education Maintenance Allowance, again a policy by Blair to help students whose parents had a low level of taxable income. It was a payment made to students who were undertaking at least 12 hours of guided learning in school sixth forms, sixth form colleges and Further Education colleges.

**Cultural capital** refers to non-financial, social elements that are associated with middle-class culture, such as knowledge of and interest in such things as the arts and current affairs.

**Speech codes** refer to elaborated and restricted codes, which are used differently by different classes.

## In-school factors

The final explanation for inequalities in educational achievement is actually a set of explanations that may fall under one heading. In-school factors are often discussed by interactionists, who broadly argue that it is what goes on within school and the education system that disadvantages working-class students. They suggest that assumptions are made about students and that a series of events may then occur as a result.

Becker argues that in the classroom, teachers interact with pupils with an 'ideal pupil' stereotype in their heads and judge students on the basis of how much they resemble this stereotype. Middle-class pupils are nearest to this ideal in terms of how they look, their behaviour, their knowledge, their speech patterns and their educational performance. This positive labelling is likely to have the practical consequence of such students being placed in top streams. In contrast, working-class pupils are furthest removed from their teacher's notion of an ideal pupil and are consequently negatively evaluated. This negative labelling is likely to have the practical consequence of more detentions, more suspensions and exclusions, and allocation to bottom sets or streams. Evidence from Rosenthal and Jacobson discovered that once labelled, students live up to these teacher judgements and a self-fulfilling prophecy occurs with pupils either succeeding or underachieving in accordance with the label.

Students are also often placed in sets, and Keddie suggests that there is a clear difference in the way in which teachers teach different sets. In her study she noted that working-class children were often in the lower sets and that these were seen as lower status and taught with much lower expectations and given access to less knowledge. Hargreaves also researched labelling in secondary modern schools, and reported the emergence of subcultures related to the labelling and setting of students. In his research he discovered that those labelled as 'difficult' or as 'non-achievers' were placed in lower sets, and those whose behaviour was more acceptable in higher ones. This limited the lower-set students' ability to achieve high status within the school, so Hargreaves argued that they sought out each other's company and formed subcultures. Within these subcultures, peers awarded high status to those who broke the school rules, creating conformist and non-conformist subcultures.

Interactionists overall discuss the micro-interactions that occur in schools between the teachers and students and suggest that these factors may combine to result in poor educational outcomes.

# Ethnicity and educational achievement

There are also differences in ethnicity and educational achievement, with certain ethnic groups doing significantly better than others. While there are many similarities between this and the explanations for class, sociologists would argue that these explanations are greater for ethnic groups due to the unique challenges they face, such as racial discrimination. There are three key explanations for this.

## Material factors

Platt argues that certain ethnic minority groups, such as Pakistanis, Bangladeshis and African Caribbeans, are more likely to live in poverty in the UK than others. This suggests that differences in achievement are not caused by cultural differences between ethnic groups, but actually by some ethnic groups being financially better

**Labelling** refers to the idea of teachers making an assumption about a student based on class, ethnicity and gender and treating them in accordance to this.

**Self-fulfilling prophecy** suggests that students live up to a label they have been given.

**Setting** is the idea of putting students into groups based on ability (or perceived ability).

**Knowledge check 22**

What are the main outside and in-school factors relating to class and achievement?

**Exam tip**

It is important to recognise that not all students from ethnic minority backgrounds are underachieving. For example, those from Indian and Chinese backgrounds tend to perform better than White students. When considering these explanations, think how they may apply differently to different ethnic groups.

off than others. Patterns of educational achievement show that Chinese, Indian and White students are the most likely to do well in school and this corresponds with the highest hourly rates of pay for male full-time employees in the UK, meaning that those who come from better-off families are more likely to be successful in school. Explanations for how money can translate to educational success (such as access to resources, etc.) can be applied in the same way as they are to social class, but it should be noted that ethnic groups who are likely to live in poverty are therefore subject to 'double disadvantage' as they are facing additional barriers pertinent to their background.

## Cultural factors

Some sociologists argue that it is cultural factors that cause differences in ethnic underachievement. For example, Sewell would suggest that African Caribbean boys are more likely to adopt an attitude of 'street' values as they place their respect on multimillion-pound rap stars. These values reject education and place importance on material goods and gangster lifestyles, creating a culture of rejection of education. Sewell suggests that the relatively high proportion of African Caribbean students raised in lone-parent families can also lead to some boys suffering due to a lack of positive male role models and the discipline that comes with this, and that the hyper-masculinity of gangs and rap culture becomes an attractive form of masculinity as a replacement, which results in a lack of respect for authority and a rejection of school.

Some sociologists have suggested that cultural factors can also have a positive effect on attainment, for example with Chinese students, who are the most successful at education. Archer and Francis would argue that the parents of Chinese children are so pro-education that they embed educational content and values into home life, along with high expectations of achievement, meaning that their children are highly successful at school.

Some more recent migrants to the UK may have unwittingly become downwardly mobile as they are unable to get jobs relevant to their skills since moving, either due to a lack of opportunity or to a lack of familiarity with British culture and systems. As a result they are living in a class position that is different to where they would ordinarily be. Modood argues that as a result of this, many ethnic minority parents may have more cultural capital (see discussion of Bourdieu, page 35), and can therefore provide more help for their children in education.

Parental attitudes towards education are also an important cultural factor. Basit suggests that British Asian communities place high value on education and see free state education as a 'blessing' as it offers more opportunities to their children than would be available in their countries of origin, so as a result they focus on supporting their children. Even those who do not have material wealth manage to provide educational resources such as study space and internet, but in turn their children are expected to work hard. Basit argues that these parents see education as the key to success and as the most significant asset a young person can acquire, so even though they cannot afford to move to catchment areas with the best schools, they are still very focused on helping their children. Basit also observes that Asian, and especially Indian, parents insist their offspring show respect to their teachers in the classroom. Consequently, it is supposedly rare that Indian children misbehave in class.

**Exam tip**

Questions may refer to 'ethnic groups', which would include White people, as they are are an ethnic group.

## In-school factors

Some sociologists argue that the reason for differences in achievement between ethnic groups is actually to do with things that go on in the education system itself.

Coard argues that one form of institutional racism present in the education system is that the curriculum itself excludes ethnic minority children from achieving their potential as it is ethnocentric and not relevant to them. By this he is suggesting that the core curriculum is written from a White British perspective and culturally only relevant to such students. For example in English, only British literature is studied rather than global literature. This may cause students to disengage and begin to fall behind.

Interactionists argue that labelling, stereotyping and subcultures are all combined factors that contribute towards the underachievement of Afro-Caribbean students. Gillborn suggests that these students are more likely to be punished or suspended than their peers, because teachers perceive their fashion, demeanour and manner of speech as representing an anti-school value. Students then live up to these labels and a self-fulfilling prophecy occurs. Jasper develops this theory, looking specifically at the teaching style of White female teachers, suggesting their conservative approach is not conducive or productive to the flamboyant and artistic learning style that Black boys may need. Connolly also notes differences in teacher attitudes towards ethnic minority students and suggests that teachers view some South Asian boys as immature rather than anti-school but that this behaviour is ignored and therefore not punished in the same way as that of Black boys.

Mirza, however, would agree that although labelling occurs, it does not always have this negative effect, particularly on Black girls. She suggests that these students are confident in their own abilities and able to ignore these labels and succeed, inferring that there is a myth of underachievement. O'Donnell agrees with Mirza, but says the difference is not dependent on gender, but on the actual ethnic group itself. He suggests that African Caribbean males often react negatively to these labels and as a result reject the White-dominated education system, whereas Indian students (who are also angered by this labelling) do not tend to reject the education system, but instead utilise it to their advantage.

According to Strand, the setting of students is another factor, linked to labelling, that creates differences between ethnic groups in education, with the suggestion that students are labelled at a young age and placed into sets in accordance to this. African Caribbean students do significantly less well in education than White British peers at the age of 14, regardless of differences in class, family, school and religion. These students are less likely to be entered for higher-level GCSEs than their peers. Gillborn extends this argument but suggests that this affects some ethnic minorities much more than others. He argues that 'model minorities', such as Chinese and Indian students, are perceived as having a positive attitude towards education so are therefore favoured, unlike Black children who are perceived as a potential problem. Gillborn also suggests that teachers unconsciously interpret policy in a way that disadvantages Black students. This is evidenced by the lack of entry for Black students into higher-tier exams. His study indicates that teachers are more likely to underrate the abilities of Black children, by placing them in low-ability groups. As a result of this a limited curriculum is taught and they are entered for only lower-level exams, creating vast differences overall at GCSE level.

**Knowledge check 23**

What are the main outside and in-school factors relating to ethnicity and achievement?

Many sociologists, however, such as Foster et al., criticise research into ethnicity and education, saying that it fails to uncover the true extent of racism and that we should take a more critical look at the system itself.

# Gender and educational achievement

Generally girls outperform boys at GCSE, but the actual picture is slightly more complex, with boys outperforming girls in some subject and girls or boys less likely to be taking certain subjects. This, however, has not always been the case, as boys used to do better than girls at this level, but overall both sexes have improved over the last three decades. Boys do, however, still outperform girls at university. There have been several explanations given for these trends.

## Changing attitudes

The feminist Sharpe argues that the values of young women have significantly changed. The emphasis used to be on girls settling down and getting married, whereas now they are far more career-minded and therefore work harder at school. This is also developed by Francis and Skelton who say that this is particularly the case for middle-class girls, who are very career-focused and have definite ideas about their future.

Sharpe's original study looked at young working-class females in London in the 1970s and found overwhelmingly that at that time most girls had traditional ideas about becoming a woman, prioritising 'love, marriage, husbands, children, jobs and careers, more or less in that order'. She then repeated this study in 1994, and discovered that their priorities had changed and now more than anything they wanted a job that would mean they could be financially independent. Supporting this is the study conducted by Francis and Skelton who researched primary school girls in 2005 and also found that career was important, and more vitally that now these students saw particular careers as key to their identity, with many aiming towards graduate jobs. Feminist sociologist Wilkinson agrees that it is changing attitudes that have had an effect on girls' educational achievement, along with a **feminisation of the economy** and the workforce. There has been an expansion of jobs for women in the service sector of the economy, giving girls more choices in terms of a career. Wilkinson suggests that there has been a **genderquake**, meaning a real shift in terms of attitudes towards women and work at the end of the twentieth century. For young women in the twenty-first century it is now more acceptable for their aspirations to be career-based. This shift of aspiration has undoubtedly played a large role in the increased attainment of girls.

## Changing landscapes

Changing economic landscapes have also had an effect on boys and educational attainment. Industry and the needs of the economy have changed significantly since the 1970s. Mac an Ghaill suggests that working-class boys are experiencing a 'crisis of masculinity'. The decline in the availability of manual work and the link this has to being a traditional breadwinner may mean that boys no longer achieve at school as they see their identity as no longer attainable. Wragg argues that young boys have become negative towards the employment opportunities available, making them reject schooling and trying hard.

**Exam tip**

Avoid making sweeping statements asserting that there is full gender equality now. It is fine to acknowledge the positive steps made towards this, but note that many inequalities still exist.

The **feminisation of the economy** refers to a rise in the service sector where women are as equally placed as men to compete for work.

**Genderquake** implies a shift in attitudes from men to women.

Changing attitudes in society went hand in hand with changes in legislation. The Equal Pay Act 1970 and the Women's Movement have not only brought about awareness of inequalities but have also sought to address the legal discrepancies between men and women. While men and women are not equal yet, these changes have brought about a greater level of aspiration, giving young women higher educational aims. It is now illegal for women not to receive equal status, pay and rights in relation to men at work, and better legal protection and rights are available for women who wish to work and also have children. It is now illegal to deny a woman the right to return to her previous work on a part-time basis after returning from maternity leave. The option of combining a career and family has undoubtedly encouraged some girls to pursue education, as a choice of one or the other is no longer necessary.

There have also been several policies introduced to try and redress gender inequalities in areas of industry such as science and engineering. Traditionally girls were less likely to take these subjects at school or progress on to have careers in them. During the time of the Conservative government of the 1980s, schemes such as GIST (Girls into Science and Technology) and the WISE campaign (Women into Science and Engineering) were launched, which attempted to encourage girls to study more male-dominated subjects. Also the introduction of coursework by the same government was said to benefit girls as they are more suited to this mode of assessment and therefore achieve more. Ofsted also assesses for diversity and inclusion in education and is very focused on eliminating sexism.

## Subject choice and in-school changes

Patterns of gender and subject choice do still remain, however, and many sociologists have researched this because subjects lead to progression, jobs and pay in later life. Skelton, Francis and Valkanova assessed when these changes begin to be evidenced and they argue that it is during Key Stage 4 (GCSE options) that differences emerge, with girls picking 'caring' subjects such as health and social care and boys picking science-based courses. This causes issues in terms of progression pathways as it limits A-level choice. Colley suggests that these choices are in part down to the influence of the family and peers, who tend to hold stereotypical views about subject choice. But she believes this is more due to the fact that teachers still hold traditional cultural beliefs about femininity and masculinity and this may be implicitly conveyed to students via teaching styles and the fact that the teachers themselves are likely to be male for the 'boys' subjects and vice versa. This then makes subject choice gendered, with males more likely to choose chemistry, physics, economics and maths and females to choose biology, English and sociology, leading to gender differences at degree level and ultimately career-level too.

There has, however, been academic debate on the true extent of the issue of gender and achievement. Coffey argues that the media has created a moral panic about gender and education. Are boys really failing as much as we think or are girls just improving and bridging the gap?

The Equal Pay Act 1970 prohibits any less favourable treatment between men and women in terms of pay and conditions of employment.

The Women's Movement is a movement campaigning for the equal rights and liberation of women.

**Knowledge check 24**

What are the main outside and in-school factors relating to gender and achievement?

# Educational inequalities in a global context

## *The global 'gender apartheid' in education*

Globally, there are significant differences in gender and education, with some women and girls being greatly disadvantaged. Feminists have called this a 'gender apartheid' and suggest it is because there are practices that prevent girls from accessing education in the same ways as boys, or in some cases at all. Attempts have been made by the **United Nations** to decrease these inequalities but statistics show that in certain countries some girls still remain in a subordinate position to boys. For example, in 2014 research by the UN showed that in Yemen, 92% of young women had not completed primary education. The UN has faced criticism from feminists such as Meyer for failing to truly address the problem, but cultural practices and values are a sensitive issue and are complex and take time to change. It is also difficult to obtain a true measurement of gender and education on a global scale.

There are several reasons for these disparities, and UNESCO (the United Nations Educational, Social and Cultural Organization) suggests that one key factor may be family expectations. Some girls are required to carry out domestic tasks as their family unit is structured to require this, while also facing the pressure of the family to remain at home due to religious and cultural beliefs. The curriculum itself may in some schools be targeted towards boys, with a focus on maths and sciences as these subjects meet the needs of that country's economy.

These statistics must be treated with caution, however, as they are collected locally and not all information can be deemed fully valid or reliable.

During the time of the Coalition government, Gove's educational policy was heavily influenced by global factors, for example, the Singapore education system which is managed financially in a unique way and seen as 'world leading', and also the marketisation of education in the USA.

The **United Nations** is an organisation that aims to maintain peace, security and human rights.

# The disparity in educational provision around the world

UNESCO's original report on inequalities in global education in 2000 outlined many differences and set clear aims for countries to improve. It highlighted that there are other types of inequalities within education in relation to poverty and ethnicity. UNESCO set out educational targets for the countries with the highest levels of educational inequalities to meet and later reported that the countries that have failed to meet those education targets are the poorest countries.

The 2016 report shows that just 64 countries of the 157 tracked by the report met one of the aims, which was for every child in the world to receive a full course of primary school education by 2015. But not a single low-income country met the target nor are any on course to do so, with Niger, Rwanda and Central African Republic being among the 11 countries not expected to achieve universal primary education until 2100.

Ethnic inequalities also occur in many countries. In America, for example, Hispanic students are the most likely not to graduate from high school, and Reardon suggests that this is possibly due to material and cultural factors and to the high levels of unemployment in the cities where they are most likely to live.

It should be recognised, however, that there are cultural differences and structures that require gender roles for the society to be functional, and in some countries such as Mongolia boys are actually taken out of school at an early age to begin work. Are the recommendations actually just a Westernised ideal? Should we really impose cultural ideas of equality on other countries?

Filmer argues that all of these types of inequality are important, however to focus on one neglects the main underlying issue of poverty.

### Summary

- Inequalities in education exist due to either structural or micro-reasons.
- Policies seek to address these inequalities.
- It is important to look at the interrelationship between class, ethnicity and gender and not to just assess each one in isolation.

**Knowledge check 25**

When was education first measured globally?

# How has the UK education system changed?

## The diversity of educational provision

### Developments in the structure and organisation of the education system since 1988

The UK has a diverse education system. Devolved power to Scotland, Northern Ireland and Wales means each organises its own system slightly differently, but even within England there are different types of schools at each stage. For example, at secondary school age, there used to be a **tripartite system** that separated students into grammar, secondary modern and technical schools, based on performance in the 11-plus examination.

The system was controversial as LEAs often spent the majority of their budget on the grammar schools, leaving the other schools in each borough as second-rate. As they were selective they tended to take the mainly middle-class students who passed the 11-plus and as a result this created a polarisation of achievement.

The tripartite system was gradually replaced by the comprehensive system from 1965 onwards, as governments switched between Labour and Conservative. Comprehensive schools did not select students in terms of ability and were open to all. By 1975 most schools had become comprehensive, though a few grammar schools remained. A law forbidding the creation of new grammar schools was passed in 1998 by Tony Blair's Labour Government (Schools Standards and Framework Act 1998).

## Types of school in England

### Community schools

In community schools the LEA is in control, appointing teachers and owning the buildings.

### Foundation schools

In foundation schools, it is the governing body that is in control. It deals with the staff and admissions, and the land is likely to be owned by a charity.

### Voluntary-aided/voluntary-controlled schools

Usually faith schools, these are owned and controlled by a charitable trust and governing body. These are responsible for the running and admissions of the school.

### Grammar schools

These still exist and select almost all of their students in relation to academic ability. There are currently just over 160 grammar schools in England, across just 11 counties. They are state-funded but selective in admission.

### Academies

This is a type of secondary school that is independent, but publicly funded and publicly run. They are often operated by one 'outstanding school' and the others work in this partnership. They are not subject to the requirements of the National Curriculum but do follow it.

The **tripartite system** existed from 1944 onwards, and put schools into three types: grammar, technical and secondary modern. Students were allocated to each type of school based on the outcome of the 11-plus exam at the end of Year 6.

**Exam tip**

Avoid 'listing' policies; always link them to the aim and theoretical underpinning, and above all relate them to the question.

## Free schools

**Knowledge check 26**

Which system largely replaced the tripartite system?

Free schools are funded by the government but are not run by the LEA and have more autonomy than other schools. They can set their own pay and conditions for staff and they do not have to follow the National Curriculum. Parents, the community and faith organisations can set up a free school.

# Government theories and policies from 1988 onwards

Each government is underpinned by a different ideological perspective, such as New Right, liberal or social democratic. While there are other influences, these perspectives have had the greatest influence overall on educational policy since 1988. Governments introduce policies into education based on these beliefs and with one or more of the following aims in mind:

- Raising standards (through competition)
- Equality of opportunity
- To meet the needs of the economy
- Diversity and choice

## Conservative governments

| Conservative Government | Overarching aims while in office |
|---|---|
| Margaret Thatcher (1979–90)<br>John Major (1990–97)<br>David Cameron (2015–16)<br>Theresa May (2016–present) | Meet the needs of the economy<br>Diversity and choice<br>Raising standards |

### Theoretical underpinning and rationale: ideology — New Right

The New Right was influenced by Buchanan and Tullock's public choice theory. They wanted educational policies to increase choice using market principles to raise standards. They believed that schools should be managed in the same way as businesses. New Right policies became increasingly influential during the Conservative governments of 1979 to 1997. In a free market, consumers have choice and the producers of these choices compete to produce the best product. In other words, it is in the interests of individual schools to compete with each other to attract students, and as a result of this competition overall standards of education will improve. The New Right also sought to meet the needs of the economy, one of which was tackling the issue of unemployment in the 1980s. The way in which Margaret Thatcher's government did this was by implementing vocational education and training, as it felt that schools were not teaching the relevant skills to facilitate young people getting jobs.

Schemes were developed to address this, for example apprenticeships and training schemes that were a combination of work and training, whereby young people worked towards achieving NVQs (National Vocational Qualifications).

The Conservatives next came into power as part of the Coalition government in 2010, but in 2015 David Cameron won a majority during the general election. Since then they have continued to develop the policies and ideology of the Coalition but with a shift towards New Right more recently under the direction of Theresa May, with proposed policies such as the reintroduction of grammar schools.

## Labour governments

| Labour (often referred to as 'New Labour') | Overarching aims while in office |
|---|---|
| Tony Blair (1997–2007)<br>Gordon Brown (2007–10) | Equality of opportunity<br>Diversity and choice<br>Raising standards |

### Theoretical underpinning and rationale: ideology — social democratic

Social democratic ideology is underpinned by a commitment to policies aimed at curbing inequality. Like Marxists and functionalists, social democrats accept that wealth and power is not equally distributed and they strongly believe the state should intervene to redress this by creating an education system that seeks to give everyone equal access and chances to succeed by offering support and initiatives to students from less advantaged backgrounds. They also argue that a key role of education is to produce a workforce that meets the needs of the economy. There are some elements of New Labour's policies that have actually supported and developed New Right/Conservative ideas, however, such as the expansion of specialist schools and academies.

## Conservative–Liberal Democrat Coalition government

| Conservative–Liberal Democrat 2010–15 | Overarching aims while in office |
|---|---|
| David Cameron<br>Nick Clegg (deputy) | Diversity and choice<br>Raising standards |

### Theoretical underpinning and rationale: ideology — New Right and social democratic

After Labour's defeat in the 2010 election, there was a Coalition government in power. Led by the Conservatives with David Cameron as Prime Minister, the supporting party was the Liberal Democrats with Nick Clegg as the Deputy Prime Minister. In order to function the policies were primarily New Right, but with some social democratic influence from the Liberal Democrats as well. David Cameron also cut several social democratic initiatives including Sure Start on the grounds of austerity.

**Knowledge check 27**

What are the two main ideological political influences?

# Education policies since 1988

| Policy | Government/ ideology | Aims | Explanations |
|---|---|---|---|
| 1988 Education Reform Act — National Curriculum | Margaret Thatcher, Conservative New Right | Equality of opportunity Meet the needs of the economy Raising standards | The intention of the Act was for standard lessons to be taught across all schools. There would be core subjects: English, maths, ICT and science, and these would be set out in key stages. |
| 1988 Education Reform Act — Open Enrolment | Margaret Thatcher, Conservative New Right | Equality of opportunity Raising standards Diversity and choice | Parents were given the choice to send children to schools other than those that were immediately local to their house. |
| 1988 Education Reform Act — SATs | Margaret Thatcher, Conservative New Right | Raising standards | Tests were Introduced at ages 7, 11 and 14 to assess students' ability and schools' performance. |
| 1988 Education Reform Act — League Tables | Margaret Thatcher, Conservative New Right | Raising standards Diversity and choice | SATs, GCSE and A-level results and truancy rates of each school were published. These were made available to everyone so parents could assess the suitability and performance of the school. |
| Introduction of Ofsted | Margaret Thatcher, Conservative New Right | Raising standards Equality of opportunity | The introduction of an organisation of inspectors who assess schools on a set of criteria. They do this by visiting the schools routinely to ensure education institutions are operating at a sufficient standard. They grade each institution on school ethos, quality of lessons, facilities and progress. |
| Introduction of Specialist Schools | John Major, Conservative New Right | Raising standards Meet the needs of the economy | Secondary schools were encouraged to become specialist in a specific area, e.g. ICT, technology, science, etc. |
| Fresh Start | Tony Blair, Labour social democrat | Raising standards | This policy was aimed at schools that were underperforming, particularly those in inner-city and deprived areas that struggled to attract experienced or good quality teachers. Failing schools would be closed and re-launched with a new name, new staff and management, and given two years to improve. |
| Excellence in Cities (EiC) 1999 | Tony Blair, Labour social democrat | Raising standards | The programme tackled underachievement in schools and promoted participation in inner-city areas, tackling disaffection, social exclusion and truancy. This was done by the introduction of Learning Mentors and Learning Support Units, and the construction of City Learning Centres (ICT resource centres for children in deprived areas to use). |
| Education Action Zones | Tony Blair, Labour social democrat | Raising standards Equality of opportunity | EAZs are areas that face social problems, such as poverty and crime, in which schools are given additional finance and resources. |

| Policy | Government/ ideology | Aims | Explanations |
|---|---|---|---|
| Literacy and Numeracy Hours | Tony Blair, Labour social democrat | Raising standards Meet the needs of the economy | Added to National Curriculum — it became compulsory that all students had to do at least one hour of English and maths each day. |
| New Deal | Tony Blair, Labour social democrat | Meet the needs of the economy | This was introduced in order to address young unemployed people. They were given training for one year or work for six months and financial support while doing so. |
| Value Added League Tables | Tony Blair, Labour social democrat | Raising standards Diversity and choice | Schools' exam results were already published but this showed the improvements the school had helped the children to make, helping assess the overall performance of the school. |
| Curriculum 2000 | Tony Blair, Labour social democrat | Diversity and choice | This was a major A-level reform that split A-levels into AS and A2. These were further split into modules with exams in January and June. There was also the introduction of more varied subjects, e.g. photography, travel and tourism, health and social care, etc. |
| Sure Start | Tony Blair, Labour social democrat | Raising standards Equality of opportunity | This was an initiative to support families from deprived areas pre-school. The emphasis was on providing educational play, and advice and support for parents. |
| Educational Maintenance Allowance (EMA) | Tony Blair, Labour social democrat | Equality of opportunity | This policy was aimed at encouraging students from poorer backgrounds into higher education by providing additional funding for transport, books, etc. |
| Personalised Learning | Tony Blair, Labour social democrat | Meet the needs of the economy Equality of opportunity Raising standards | Provide people aged 19+ with 80% of costs for training schemes of their choice. Basing education around the individual's needs and interests, the aim was to allow young people to tailor their educational needs rather than be restricted to courses offered. |
| HE Tuition Fees | Tony Blair, Labour social democrat | Equality of opportunity Raising standards | The Government introduced fees of £3000 per year in order to maintain quality degree provision, but with grants and concessions available for poorer students. |
| 14–19 Reform | Tony Blair, Labour social democrat | Meet the needs of the economy Diversity and choice | Although this was never actually implemented in full, the idea was to raise the school leaving age to 18 and to introduce a new Diploma that combined vocational and academic studies together. |
| 2000 — City Academy Schools | Tony Blair, Labour social democrat | Diversity and choice Raising standards | Failing secondary schools in deprived areas would be 'rebranded' as City Academies. |
| 2010 — Expansion of Academy Schools | David Cameron/Nick Clegg, Coalition New Right/liberal | Diversity and choice Raising standards | This policy widened academy eligibility. Primary schools could now take part as well as secondary. |

| Policy | Government/ ideology | Aims | Explanations |
|---|---|---|---|
| 2010 — Introduction of Free Schools | David Cameron/Nick Clegg, Coalition New Right/liberal | Diversity and choice | This policy allowed members of a community and parents to apply to set up their own school where there is currently a shortage of school places. Open to all students. |
| Increase in HE Tuition Fees | David Cameron/Nick Clegg, Coalition New Right/liberal | Equality of opportunity Raising standards Meet the needs of the economy | University tuition fees rose to £9000 per year. Tuition fee loans were offered to all. Grants and additional loans were offered to lower income students. |
| Proposed Changes to National Curriculum | David Cameron/Nick Clegg, Coalition New Right/liberal | Meet the needs of the economy Raising standards | The Government proposed several changes to the current National Curriculum, such as: <br>• Introduction of languages earlier in schools (KS2). <br>• Replacing ICT with computing. <br>• Greater emphasis on spelling, grammar and vocabulary. |
| Changes to GCSE | David Cameron/Nick Clegg, Coalition New Right/liberal | Raising standards | This policy changed the structure of assessment, and removed coursework and controlled assessment. It also removed modules — with a final exam at the end of two years. |
| Changes to A-level | David Cameron/Nick Clegg, Coalition New Right/liberal | Raising standards | This policy completely changed A-levels too, with the abolition of AS and A2, separate modules and coursework. The qualification became a two-year linear course with final exams at the end of two years. |
| Removal/Reduction of Sure Start, EMA, etc. | David Cameron/Nick Clegg, Coalition New Right/liberal | | This policy reversed some of New Labour's support initiatives. |
| Introduction of Pupil Premium | David Cameron/Nick Clegg, Coalition New Right/liberal | Equality of opportunity | This gave schools extra funding for each child from a deprived area, to spend on extra facilities to support them. |
| Phonics Testing | David Cameron/Nick Clegg, Coalition New Right/liberal | Raising standards | This is a method of teaching and testing 'phonetic awareness', teaching young children to identify and manipulate sounds and spelling patterns. It was introduced as part of the core curriculum in an attempt to raise literacy standards. |
| Changes to the Curriculum | David Cameron, Conservative New Right | Raising standards | Slimming down of the curriculum as a whole for ages 5–18. The breadth of subjects offered was reduced, with a greater focus on the more 'traditional' subjects. The qualifications themselves were rewritten in phases between 2014 and 2016 to make them more academic and rigorous. |
| Proposed Reintroduction of Grammar Schools | Theresa May, Conservative New Right | Raising standards | The proposed reintroduction of grammar schools in order to raise standards of education, allowing selection of students to ensure they get specialist, academic educational opportunities. |

Educational policies also have an impact on achievement in relation to class, gender and ethnicity. In relation to social class, there are clear attempts to create equality of opportunity as outlined above, but the divide in achievement between classes remains, with only 32.3% of White British children who receive free school meals achieving 5 GCSE (A–C) passes, as opposed to 64.5% of White British children who do not (DfE, 2014). Attempts were made to address these differences by New Labour policies such as Sure Start, but this divide does still remain. Marxists would argue that the structure of the system itself disadvantages working-class children and that no matter what policy is introduced, the system itself must be changed and not based around a capitalist economy in order to truly address the differences.

Policy has sought to address the differences between the achievements of girls and boys, with initiatives such as GIST and WISE targeting young women to encourage participation in male-dominated industries. Additionally, all children must now study the same curriculum regardless of gender, meaning that they have an equal foundation in such subjects. The introduction of coursework has also contributed to the rise in girls' achievement. Some would argue, however, that this has all been to the detriment of boys, and subsequently more recent policies have sought to look at the underachievement of White working-class boys.

Differences still occur in terms of educational achievement and ethnicity. Despite attempts to broaden the curriculum through the introduction of the idea of multicultural education, sociologists argue that it remains ethnocentric and focused on the White majority. New Labour's re-evaluation of the use of religious education in schools did attempt to address this focus; while RE was made compulsory in education, LEAs were able to set their own demographically specific curriculum — this was unlike other subjects that were nationally controlled. Also, the introduction of free schools and academies has benefited certain ethnic groups, with the attainment of Bangladeshi children significantly increasing because schools in the areas where they were populated were often deprived and were improved as a result of the introduction of free schools and academies.

**Exam tip**

It is fine to evaluate the failings of a policy or government by talking about what was implemented after, but for top AO1 marks use additional knowledge such as links to theories like Marxism or feminism.

**Knowledge check 28**

What have been the four main aims of governments in relation to educational policy since 1988?

---

## Summary

- All governments broadly work towards the four aims of: creating diversity and choice; improving equality of opportunity; meeting the needs of the economy; and raising standards. They all agree these are important but focus on different things at different times depending on their ideology and on factors specific to the time of decision-making.
- Policies often seek to address social, vocational and educational inequalities and issues brought about by previous policies.
- To a certain extent many of these policies have not really been successful, as there are still inequalities in achievement between certain groups.
- Recent Conservative-led governments have shown themselves to be more similar to the Conservative governments of the 1980s and 1990s in their ideological position, compared to the Labour government which came in between.

# Questions & Answers

## How to use this section

In this section you will find three questions at A-level. Each has an A-grade answer with comments on each answer at the end, stating why it gained the marks it did, and what improvements, if any, could be made. The question numbering for the A-level questions is the same as you will find in the examination.

You should read each question carefully, and either try to answer it in full or at least make notes of how you would answer it *before* reading the student answer and comments. This might help to pick up on mistakes you have made or things that you are doing well. Remember that there is no single perfect way of answering an exam question — the highest marks can be gained by taking different approaches, especially in the higher-mark questions. However, the comments should help to show you the kinds of approach that would do well, and some of the pitfalls to avoid.

As a general point, you should always read through the whole question before starting to write. When you come to answer the question that is based on a source, read the source particularly carefully, as it will contain material that is essential to answering the question.

Examiner comments on the questions are preceded by the icon **e** and give hints and guidance on how to answer the question. The candidate answers are also accompanied by comments. These are preceded by the icon **e** and indicate where credit is due. The comments tell you what it is that enables the candidate to score so highly. Particular attention is given to the candidate's use of the examinable skills or Assessment Objectives (AOs): AO1, knowledge and understanding (including range and depth of relevant sociological evidence); AO2, application (relating to how well focused the answer is, and/or how well the source has been applied); and AO3, analysis and evaluation (relating to criticisms and challenges to the view in the question, and including a reasoned conclusion for some questions). You should already be familiar with these from your other two components.

# The A-level examination

The topic of 'Debates in contemporary society' is examined on Paper 3 of the A-level examination, which is organised into two sections. Section A, which is compulsory, focuses on 'Globalisation and the digital social world' and contains two sources. Both sources contain information about aspects of the topic. In questions 1 and 2, reference must be made to at least one of the sources to access the highest A02 marks, in addition to using wider sociological knowledge where appropriate. Question 3 will depend solely on your wider sociological knowledge. Section A questions add up to 35 marks altogether or 33% of the paper.

Section B comprises questions on the three optional units. This guide focuses on one of these — Education — which is Option 2. It contains three questions, which must all be answered and which are worth 10, 20 and 40 marks respectively. Section B questions therefore add up to 70 marks altogether or 67% of the paper.

The whole exam lasts for 2 hour 15 minutes, carries 105 marks and is worth 35% of the A-level qualification. It is worth spending about 45 minutes on Section A and 90 minutes on Section B. Try to manage your time so that you have enough spare to read through your responses to the whole paper at the end.

## Question 1

Section A

*Globalisation and the digital social world*

**Read the source material and answer all the questions in Section A.**

> **Source A**
>
> Globalisation is the term used to refer to the integration of goods, services and culture among the nations of the world. Advances in telecommunication technologies have particularly accelerated globalisation. In 2012, the internet was being used in over 150 countries by 2.4 billion people worldwide. From the development of the World Wide Web in the 1990s to the social networks and e-commerce of today, the internet has continued to increase integration between countries, making globalisation a fact of life for citizens all over the world.

> **Source B**
>
> As the digital revolution continues to spread across the world, it is also creating a separation between those who have access to this global network and those who do not. This digital divide is causing great concern. Certain social categories — low-income households, senior citizens, children from lone-parent families, the undereducated and underqualified and members of ethnic minority groups — are prevented from receiving fair access to digital communication technology. Moreover, this digital divide can also occur between regions in the same country. There is also a global digital divide. For example, although mobile phone technology has dramatically expanded in Africa, broadband connections are extremely poor compared with Western societies.

**1** **With reference to the sources, explain how digital communications have contributed to the process of globalisation.** [9 marks]

ⓔ You must make clear reference to at least one of the sources as well as your wider knowledge.

**2** With reference to the sources, to what extent has the digital divide weakened the idea that the world has experienced a digital revolution? [10 marks]

(e) You need to supplement reference to at least one of the sources with your wider knowledge. The phrase 'to what extent' means you are expected to include some evaluation of the statement.

**3** Evaluate the view that the world has become a global village characterised by cultural homogeneity or sameness. [16 marks]

(e) The third question in Section A of the exam may well ask you to evaluate/ discuss or assess a 'view'. The 'view' may refer to a theoretical view, or a particular side in a debate. Identify the theory and/or evidence which supports the view and then explain it. Evaluation requires discussion of strengths and weaknesses, and using evidence that challenges the view presented.

## Section B

**Answer all the questions in Section B.**

*Education*

**4** In what ways can it be argued that there is a global 'gender apartheid' in education? [10 marks]

(e) 10-mark questions don't require evaluation. In a question like this, however, evidence about an issue can be presented critically and be credited as knowledge and understanding of the issues involved. Note also that in some areas of the specification, such as this, there may be fewer studies to learn and evidence may come more from statistics and international research, as well as from examples.

**5** Assess social democratic views on the role of education. [20 marks]

(e) Though this question is about the role of education, using policies to illustrate how education may perform this role is acceptable. Remember that the term 'assess' requires evaluation using other views, but that the focus should remain on the view in the question.

**6** Outline and evaluate sociological explanations for differences in educational achievement between ethnic groups. [40 marks]

(e) This is a wide-ranging question, requiring you to discuss a range of different explanations, which gives a lot of scope for range of knowledge. Be careful not to forget to explicitly evaluate each explanation, rather than just presenting various competing views.

## Student answer

### Section A

1 Globalisation means that the world we live in feels smaller and is more interconnected. A huge contributor to this are advances in digital communication which mean that geographical distance and time are no longer important. Harvey argues that this space–time compression is the most important aspect of globalisation. The internet, e-mails, texting and smartphones have transformed relationships across the world because information can be transmitted instantaneously to all destinations at all times.

Source A suggests that the internet has, at the very least, accelerated the pace of globalisation. In the pre-digital age, communication usually meant coming into contact with physical things such as people, letters, newspapers or telephones. In contrast, communication in the digital age is no longer constrained by the physical. It can now take place instantly in cyberspace via e-mails, Skype messaging, social networking sites such as Facebook and Twitter and virtual communities. Source A provides evidence of the global use of the internet — pointing out that it is used in over 150 countries, which clearly increases integration between countries.

Some sociologists are very excited by the relationship between globalisation and digital technology because they argue that it has resulted in a participatory global culture in which the people of the world can share their experiences, share cultural ideas about personal identity and provide social capital in the form of support networks.

More negatively, globalisation has been viewed as an unequal process, for example by Marxists, in the sense that it often involves richer nations imposing their culture on poorer ones: a form of cultural imperialism. This links to Source B, which refers to the global digital divide. This could imply that digital communications have contributed to globalisation by spreading Western cultural ideas globally, and that as the access to these is also unequal, global inequality is furthered.

⊜ This answer shows excellent understanding of the question, and is very focused. It shows good use of both sources, describes more than one view and is backed up with wider sociological evidence. Note that it is not necessary to use both sources to gain full marks, but one of them must be used explicitly. **9/9 marks awarded (AO1 5/5, AO2 4/4).**

**2** One of the key ideas about the world experiencing a digital revolution is that it is a democratic process and information is freely available to all, creating a global village. It is argued that digital technology has transformed the relationship between ordinary people and political elites, and that the internet in particular contains all the knowledge required to challenge the power of the state by organising global collective action.

Castells talks about a networked global society in which the politically motivated are increasingly going online and organising via social media such as Twitter and Facebook. Information is also freely available to all via sites such as Wikipedia, while sites such as WikiLeaks have allowed ordinary people to read about the secrets kept from people by governments across the world.

However, the idea that there has been a global digital revolution is undermined by inequalities in access and use of digital technology. There is a digital divide, which is discussed in Source B. This means that many people are unable to participate in this networked global society. Helsper notes that in the UK access to the internet, broadband and smartphones is often not possible for poorer sections of society such as the long-term unemployed, pensioners and the poor. These ideas are supported by Source B, which also highlights other groups who may be part of this digital underclass, including children from lone-parent families, the undereducated and underqualified, and members of ethnic minority groups. Consequently internet and smartphone use is mainly dominated by the middle classes.

However, the biggest digital divide, referred to in Source B as the global digital divide, is that which can be seen between countries. In 2014, 4 billion people, almost 60% of the world's population, had no access to the internet. The use of digital technology is dominated by Western societies because these countries are mainly responsible for the design of the software and the construction of networking sites. Moreover, most of the internet is in English, which is going to disadvantage those who do not speak English as a first language.

There is a huge digital divide between Africa and the West. Broadband and wireless access is very poor across Africa. Only a fifth of Africans had access to a smartphone in 2016 and only 7% of Africans can get online.

In conclusion, though the digital revolution has had a global impact and changed the way in which we interact, it has clearly not affected the whole world in the same way, so it is significantly undermined by problems with the digital divide.

**ⓔ** The student has written a well-organised answer, which explores a number of ways in which the digital divide has undermined a digital revolution, drawing from the source and elsewhere. A succinct conclusion rounds it off. **10/10 marks awarded (AO1 4/4, AO2 2/2, AO3 4/4).**

**3**  The idea of cultural sameness was originally identified by McLuhan, who even before the digital revolution was anxious that the globalisation of media, especially Hollywood films, was producing cultural homogeneity. Modern-day theories of globalisation share this concern. Seabrook, for example, argues that globalisation is a form of cultural imperialism which uses digital forms of communication to impose the same cultural ideas and products on the minds and everyday behaviour of the people of very different societies. It can be said that globalisation is actually Westernisation or even Americanisation, and that all cultures are becoming clones of US culture.

Marxists too are very concerned about cultural sameness and see it as a form of cultural imperialism through which capitalist ideology is spread. They argue that globalisation has been going on for centuries and is an aspect of the logic of capitalism, which is always attempting to expand its markets in search of profit. From a Marxist perspective, digital forms of communication have speeded up this process and created the mistaken impression that the power of individuals is being increased. Cornford and Robins argue that digital media is owned and controlled by a few large companies which present a uniform set of conservative values.

Marxists agree that cultural imperialism is a problem, seeing it as a form of ideology which aims to encourage consumption of Western cultural products and so distract attention away from the inequalities that tend to accompany capitalism in terms of wealth and income. So from this perspective, the media, including digital media, can be seen as one of Althusser's ideological state apparatuses, a tool to maintain ideological control. McChesney claims that social networking sites have colonised the minds of people across the world in order to encourage consumption of Western cultural and digital products and this has crowded out local cultural products. Marxists believe that this cultural sameness is a problem because it encourages conformity and false consciousness, which help to suppress protest and dissent.

However, Hall recognised that an alternative response to globalisation may be cultural resistance or defence. Some argue that some societies such as France, Iran and China have used digital technology to defend their cultures from global, and especially Western, influences although China can be criticised for overprotecting its citizens because it controls all search engines and censors web content. Iran closely monitors social media use and in 2015 prosecuted and imprisoned several young people who had uploaded to the internet a video of themselves dancing to Pharrell Williams's 'Happy'. However, there is also evidence that Africans across the continent are using digital media in culturally supportive and defensive ways in business, healthcare, education and agriculture. The reaction against homogenisation does not always come from governments. Many individuals and groups within societies may also feel uneasy about globalisation and the loss of cultural distinctiveness which it is perceived to entail, and may react in a culturally defensive way. This could partly explain the vote to leave the EU in the UK in 2016.

Other sociologists note that the power of digital media to impose cultural sameness is exaggerated. Cultural globalisation is often mistaken for full-blown globalisation but there is little sign that traditional cultural institutions such as religions and families are being overwhelmed by global influences. They point out that cultural traffic is two way rather than one way and that Western societies have benefited from the cultures of other societies — for example, Asian culture has had a significant influence on British culture. Many cultures are only selectively influenced by global culture. They select what pleases them and adapt it to local needs. This localisation, or glocalisation, produces a hybridised popular culture — for example, local people may prefer a mixture of locally and globally produced music, and local musicians may fuse these genres into new forms.

In conclusion, the argument that the global village is characterised by cultural homogeneity is only partially true. The distinct aspects of cultures around the world are still clearly evident, which many would see as a good thing, though cultural differences can also create problems.

🄮 This answer displays very good knowledge and understanding, which is well applied to the question. A well-balanced debate is created, with both sociological evidence and contemporary examples. **16/16 marks awarded (AO1 4/4, AO2 4/4, AO3 8/8).**

## Section B

4    Globally, women and girls are denied equal access to education. Feminists argue that this disadvantage is a form of 'gender apartheid', and Mayer suggests that less has been done about this than about racial apartheid, reflecting patriarchal attitudes. In 2000, the UNESCO Education for All campaign had a target to achieve gender equality in education by 2015, which has not been met. Recently, however, there's been more attention on this issue because of Malala Yousafzai, who was campaigning for the right to an education for girls in Pakistan and was shot by the Taliban in 2012. She is now a global campaigner on the issue.

There is global inequality in access to education for both genders, but it particularly affects girls for many different reasons, often cultural and religious. Traditionally, all societies, including Western societies, have given preference to boys in terms of education, but moves towards equality have not happened at the same pace globally. One inequality is the age at which girls are expected to leave education, either to take on domestic work or to marry and raise children. In Yemen, 92% of girls don't complete primary school, which is double the figure for boys. Similarly, in Kenya, domestic pressures often mean girls have less time and interest to devote to schooling. Nevertheless, in most countries, enrolment rates for both girls and boys have shown a steady upward trend and the gender gap is narrowing. For example, in parts of Asia and sub-Saharan Africa there has been a significant growth in school enrolments, and the enrolment rates for girls rose faster than those for boys.

Gender apartheid in education has a significant impact on the future lives of women. VSO data on Africa suggests that a girl who receives an education is three times less likely to get HIV and AIDS. Additionally, an extra year of secondary school can increase a woman's wages by 15–25%. Even in the West, however, although girls often do better than boys in education, they still earn less on average than men in the workforce, and this is also true in developing countries. The issue is clearly very complex, and other issues such as subject choice, status and role models are also significant.

**e** This is a comprehensive response that shows a clear understanding of the term 'gender apartheid' and provides evidence to support it, recognising some of the issues involved. Using statistics, a contemporary example and linking to feminism is enough to make this a top mark response. **10/10 marks awarded (AO1 6/6, AO2 4/4).**

**5** The social democratic approach to the role of education has similarities with both Marxism and functionalism, coming somewhere in the middle. Like Marxists, social democrats accept that wealth and power are not distributed equally, and so they believe the state should help the disadvantaged and create equality. The role of education is crucial in this, and schools should be free and available to everyone. The expansion of state education after the Second World War was based on these principles. Additionally, like functionalists, social democrats argue that a key role of education is to produce a well-trained and qualified workforce. They support greater funding of education, for these two reasons: it will ensure equality of opportunity, social mobility and fairness, and it will also benefit the economy in the long term, creating a more competitive and skilled workforce.

To achieve equality of opportunity in education and to avoid wastage of talent, social democrats support the comprehensive system, rather than the selective tripartite system that they argue favoured the middle class. Comprehensive schools provide more equality of opportunity by giving all students access to the same education. Social democrats see education as a crucial engine of social mobility, allowing any child to move up the class ladder by gaining good qualifications and a higher-paid job. They argue that material disadvantage should not lead to educational disadvantage, and that where education is not free, for example at university level, there should be grants to help those who can't afford it.

Marxists such as Althusser, however, would see social democrats as too optimistic. They would argue that, in a capitalist society, the education system is part of the ideological state apparatus and will never operate in a democratic way or provide a level playing field. Social democrats accept that the current system is not perfect, and they don't agree with functionalists that education runs meritocratically. They do have a positive view that education can be a great leveller, however, but argue that the system should be reformed further to become more meritocratic.

Halsey argues that social class inequalities in access to equal education still exist, and social democrats like him would criticise policies such as marketisation and competition in education, which the New Right favour. This is because working-class families will have less cultural and social capital and will therefore not be able to play the system as effectively, leading to disadvantage. Compensatory education schemes, such as Sure Start, introduced by Blair's Labour government, fit much more closely with social democratic views, since if education is to provide equal opportunities, there must be a level playing field to start off with. Social democrats see helping children from disadvantaged backgrounds to catch up as a key role of education, making up for cultural deprivation experienced in the family. Other schemes that provided more money and resources to schools in disadvantaged areas, such as Education Action Zones, would also have been supported by social democrats.

In evaluation, Marxists would argue these policies are just window-dressing, and will not be effective unless the underlying inequalities in society are addressed. Bowles and Gintis argue that meritocracy is a myth, and by supporting policies that give the appearance of improving equal opportunities, social democrats are just supporting the ideology that the education system can be fair. At the opposite end of the spectrum, the New Right and functionalists would also disagree with the social democratic view on the role of education. They suggest that there is a difference between equality of opportunity, which education does provide, and equality of outcome, which is not possible or desirable. If some children do badly in education, it is because of their lack of ability and effort, and schools should not try to compensate for that. Social democratic policies such as comprehensive schools and mixed ability teaching have been criticised for driving down standards for all students, and the New Right would argue that good students should be supported rather than penalised and that competition should be encouraged. There is also evidence that additional spending on education does not actually improve the economy or lead to more equality, and many policies supported by social democrats (such as Sure Start and EMA, which helped students from disadvantaged backgrounds stay on in school) have been scrapped or cut back due to lack of evidence that they were effective.

In conclusion, the social democratic approach has proved influential in affecting educational policies in recent years but, as social democrats like Halsey accept, there are still many inequalities within education that make it difficult to assess whether their ideas on the ideal role of education could ever be achieved.

ⓔ This is an excellent, full mark answer, showing detailed understanding of the social democratic view, with good links to policies to illustrate its ideas. There is also a reflective conclusion, and evaluation is sustained throughout. Note that presenting alternative views and assuming they will count as evaluation is a common mistake students make — in this response, the views of Marxists, functionalists and the New Right are used to explicitly challenge the social democratic views, rather than just described separately. **20/20 marks awarded (AO1 8/8, AO2 4/4, AO3 8/8).**

**6** There are clear differences in achievement based on ethnicity. Some ethnic groups, such as Chinese and Indian, do better than the average at GCSE and A-level. Others, such as African Caribbean, do worse. White British students' achievement is usually taken as the average to compare other ethnic groups to, but within the White British ethnic group there is also underachievement, with White working-class boys doing the worst. This suggests that ethnicity intersects with gender and social class as well. There is also evidence that some ethnic groups are less likely to stay on in higher education, or to achieve more in an FE college once they have left school. There are various explanations for these differences.

One explanation given for ethnic differences in achievement is cultural factors. Chinese parents have been found to be very focused on education, and Archer and Francis argue that their high expectations affect their children's achievement. The term 'tiger mums' has been used to describe Chinese mothers who push their children to do well. This contrasts with arguments from Tony Sewell who suggests that African Caribbean families are more likely to be single mothers, and that without a father figure Black boys in particular will often have low aspirations and lack a male role model. Sewell's views are supported by the views of the New Right, which argue that socialisation and family background can lead to Black boys underachieving and becoming deviant.

Strand challenges this, arguing that families of all ethnic minority groups, including African Caribbean, have high aspirations and place a high value on education as a way out of poverty. He does suggest that attitudes in White working-class families, who may be disillusioned with the education system due to their own experiences, can help explain White working-class underachievement. Therefore, according to Strand, other explanations, such as school experiences, might be more relevant to explain the underachievement of some ethnic minority groups. Another criticism of cultural explanations is that they are blaming the minority groups for their underachievement, rather than focusing on racism as the cause.

Another out-of-school explanation may be material rather than cultural factors — lack of resources, poorer living conditions and also the area a family lives in and the school they go to, may all have an impact on achievement, and the lower achieving ethnic groups also tend to be materially deprived. The gap between disadvantaged White students and more well-off White students, however, is much bigger than it is for ethnic minority students. This suggests that it may be a mixture of cultural and material factors that combines to affect educational achievement. Modood argues that many immigrant families live in poverty in the UK, but actually have high cultural capital based on previous education and jobs in their native countries. This means that compared to poor White families, they actually have an advantage when it comes to supporting their children's education.

Views that focus on material and cultural factors have been challenged by sociologists who argue that in-school factors have much more of an impact on educational performance. Coard argues that the curriculum is ethnocentric, focusing on White British culture and history, which can make ethnic minority students feel excluded. Many ethnic minorities do really well in education, however, so this argument is less convincing, and the curriculum is now much more multicultural anyway. Interactionists focus on the labelling process, which can lead to self-fulfilling prophecy, where students take on board the label and live up to it. Teacher labelling based on stereotypical and even racist views has been discovered by Gillborn and Youdell. Expectations of the behaviour of Black students led to greater focus on discipline rather than achievement, for example. Wright found that teachers felt Black boys were more outgoing and physical than White boys, and when unacceptable classroom behaviour was challenged, the boys were quick to accuse teachers of racism, leading to a difficult relationship between White teachers and Black students.

Mirza found that Black girls also felt they were underestimated by teachers, which caused them to feel resentful. Sometimes, though, this could lead them to try harder to prove the teachers wrong, which shows that the self-fulfilling prophecy doesn't always happen. Asian students are labelled differently due to different stereotypes according to sociologists, for example Asian students, particularly girls, are ignored by teachers, based on stereotypical assumptions that they won't understand English or won't want to speak in front of the class. These studies are outdated now, though.

Student subcultures are another explanation for ethnic differences, and they bring in parts of cultural but also in-school factors. For example, Mac an Ghaill found that Black boys formed an anti-school subculture, the Rastaheads, which was a resistance to racist labelling from teachers. They didn't value academic success and were openly defiant. A group of Asian boys, the Warriors, however, were just as resistant as the Rastaheads, but the teachers didn't perceive them to be as bad, showing that teacher labelling can be linked to student subcultures. Sewell also discusses Black boys forming subcultures, but looks at the contribution of popular culture to this, including rap stars. Their attachment to being cool and stylish often led to confrontations with teachers about uniform. White working-class boys also form anti-school subcultures, rejecting academic achievement as irrelevant and feminine, according to Willis and more recently Frosh, so these arguments may be more to do with gender and masculinity than just ethnicity.

In conclusion, there are clearly many influences on the differential achievement in different ethnic groups, and it is likely that it is a mix of cultural and in-school factors, but also that ethnicity intersects with class and gender. Functionalists would argue that the education system is meritocratic, so that any differences in achievement are down to ability and effort rather than structural causes such as racism in the system.

(e) This response is very wide-ranging, and includes evaluation throughout. It lacks depth in places, however — it would have been better to describe some of the studies mentioned, such as Sewell or Mirza, in more detail. It is better to go for slightly fewer ideas described in depth, than to deal with a huge range of ideas more superficially. Some of the evaluation points also require more development. For example, saying that studies are dated is a relevant point but needs to be expanded to explain what may be different today and why the study may not still hold true. A reflective conclusion is included. **33/40 marks awarded (AO1 13/16, AO2 7/8, AO3 13/16).**

(e) **Overall, the student scored 98 marks out of the 105 available.**

# Question 2

Section A

*Globalisation and the digital social world*

**Read the source material and answer all the questions in Section A.**

---

**Source A**

Denise Carter has investigated how geographically distant individuals are coming together on the internet to inhabit new kinds of social spaces or virtual communities. She argues that people construct and live in these new virtual worlds in ways that suggest that the internet is no longer a cyberspace distinct and separate from the real world. She conducted ethnographic research by entering CyberCity, a virtual community on the net. She found that cyberspace is just another place for people to meet and that CyberCity participants are investing as much effort in maintaining relationships as in other social spaces. She concludes that this widens the web of human relationships rather than weakening them.

---

**Source B**

The postmodernist thinker Carl Raschke believes that the increasing availability of digital communications has changed the nature of knowledge. He argues that grand narratives which were written by powerful groups which explained how the world worked in the modern age are now being abandoned in the postmodern world. He argues that the rapid spread of digital communication, particularly the internet, has created a digital university in which knowledge is now available to all because of participatory digital communities such as Wikipedia, Twitter and Facebook. He argues that knowledge in the postmodern world is hyper-knowledge because it has expanded knowledge and social capital to the previously powerless and muted. However, Marxists are sceptical and claim digital knowledge is mainly ideological and very much the product of the ruling capitalist class.

---

**1** **With reference to the sources, explain how virtual communities widen the web of human relationships.**

[9 marks]

(e) You must make clear reference to at least one of the sources as well as your wider knowledge.

**2** With reference to the sources, assess the view that digital communications have improved the situation of the 'powerless and muted'? [10 marks]

*ⓔ* You need to supplement reference to at least one of the sources with your wider knowledge. The term 'assess' means you are expected to include some evaluation of the statement.

**3** Evaluate the feminist approach to digital communication. [16 marks]

*ⓔ* The feminist view needs to be described and explained. Evaluation requires discussion of its strengths and weaknesses, ideally using other theories such as Marxism and postmodernism.

## Section B

**Answer all the questions in Section B.**

### Education

**4** In what ways is education linked to the workplace? [10 marks]

*ⓔ* This question does not require evaluation but it would be appropriate to present a range of ways, reflecting different theoretical viewpoints on the link between education and the workplace.

**5** Discuss the view that recent educational policies have increased equality of opportunity in education. [20 marks]

*ⓔ* It is important to select appropriate policies for this question, since the focus is on increasing equality of opportunity. Policies that have not done this could be used as evaluation. Additionally, different viewpoints may see policies in different ways.

**6** Outline and evaluate the importance of school factors as an explanation of differential educational achievement in relation to social class. [40 marks]

*ⓔ* Always stay focused on the question set, rather than one that you may have practised previously. So in this question it is school factors that should be the focus, and also social class, rather than other explanations of differential educational achievement that may have been learned.

| Student answer |
| --- |

### Section A

**1** In Source A, Carter argues that geographical distance is no longer important in preventing people from maintaining relationships or forming communities because people can now construct new kinds of social spaces and relationships in cyberspace. She calls these 'virtual communities'. Her research found that people who used CyberCity regarded themselves as a real community despite being physically separated from each other. Their participation in this virtual community was viewed in much the same way as their participation in their schools or workplaces. They spent as much effort maintaining their virtual relationships in CyberCity as they did with their relationships with their school friends or workmates. In other words, their online friendships were regarded as having the same value as their offline relationships, but with fewer barriers, thus widening people's network of social relationships.

Boellstorff, who researched the virtual community known as Second Life, found that disabled people who were confined to their homes by their physical impairment were able to widen their web of relationships by adopting avatar identities in Second Life.

Sociologists such as Miller argue that virtual communities such as Facebook are good for widening relationships because they are participatory cultures. They connect people to one another. Gardner and Davis, for example, observe that internet-enabled digital devices such as smartphones have widened relationships because they can transcend distance and allow for instantaneous communication. Young people, in particular, have taken advantage of such technology to the extent that Gardner and Davis suggest that young people today 'hang around' the net in the same way that previous generations hung around street corners or cafes.

Such communities also help isolated or shy individuals with low self-esteem relate to others because they lower barriers to communication.

ⓔ This answer demonstrates excellent knowledge and understanding, providing evidence which is relevant to the question, with good use of Source A. More focus on the question would have improved the answer further. **8/9 marks awarded (AO1 5/5, AO2 3/4).**

2  Postmodernists such as Raschke in Source B believe that digital communication has the potential to bring about social and political change especially for those who have traditionally been powerless and deprived of a voice, that is, groups who have deliberately been kept muted by the powerful. He argues that the internet in particular has transformed society's relationship with knowledge which in the past was always controlled by the powerful. Raschke argues that in the postmodern age people have grown tired of these old metanarratives of knowledge and are abandoning all trust in them in favour of participatory and democratic, digitally based communities such as Wikipedia, Twitter and Facebook, in which anybody can contribute to the sum of knowledge. He argues that the internet is a digital university in which knowledge is available to all and is being used by the previously powerless and muted to change their social conditions. Raschke refers to the knowledge available on the internet as 'hyper-knowledge' because it has extended our understanding of how the world works, it is freely available to all and it is not censored by the powerful.

Similarly, Castells argues that civil society is now better served by digital global networks which have the potential to become an alternative source of knowledge and political power that can challenge traditional sources of power such as the state. He argues that these networks have been used to successfully organise worldwide protests against global capitalism, while Kassim argues that the knowledge provided by Twitter, Facebook and YouTube played a major role in bringing down repressive dictators during the Arab Spring protests. Feminists too have argued that women were once a muted group but now use the internet to organise against misogyny and patriarchy through websites such as Everyday Sexism.

However, there are a number of criticisms which challenge the idea that digital communications have improved the situation of the powerless and muted. First, evidence suggests a digital divide exists in terms of access to digital communications. For example, only 7% of people in Africa have access to the internet. Second, Marxists observe that ownership of digital communications is mainly concentrated in the hands of transnational corporations. These companies have engaged in political censorship in collaboration with nation-states. For example, China has conspired with Google to make sure its citizens cannot freely access all the knowledge on the worldwide web. Finally, Curran argues that digital communications played a relatively minor role in the Arab Spring protests — it was deep-seated economic and religious factors that brought people onto the streets, not Twitter.

🅮 This is a well-argued response which provides evidence for and against the idea that muted groups have more voice as a result of digital communication. Source B is well used along with several relevant contemporary examples and there is clear evidence of evaluation. **10/10 marks awarded (AO1 4/4, AO2 2/2, AO3 4/4).**

**3**  Feminist theory is interested in analysing and explaining the persistence of patriarchy, that is, the fact that men dominate positions of power while women generally occupy second-class subordinate positions in society. There are three broad strands of feminism which can be applied.

Radical feminists argue that both old forms of media such as newspapers and magazines as well as newer digital forms of communication are engaged in three related processes. First, they are involved in a process that radical feminists call the symbolic annihilation of women. This means that media content, both digital and non-digital, show women in narrow and limited ways that send out the message that their achievements are less important than their bodies and looks. For example, radical feminists would point to the popularity of pornography on the internet, in which women's bodies are exploited for the gaze of men as evidence that digital media are merely reinforcing patriarchal and misogynistic attitudes.

Second, radical feminists argue that the media have deliberately silenced women to the extent that they are a muted group. Examples would include 'slut shaming' and the misogynistic abuse levelled at women who speak out on the internet. The recent campaign to 'Reclaim the internet', inspired by the feminist 'Reclaim the Night' movement, recognises the problem of misogyny on the net and is seeking to address it.

Third, radical feminists argue that what access women do get to the internet seems to reflect and therefore reinforce traditional feminine roles in a patriarchal society. Green and Singleton suggest that the online communities that are most popular with women users — Mumsnet and Facebook — might merely reinforce the patriarchal notion that women should perform the emotional work of maintaining family relationships. However, they are more positive about the female use of smartphones and texting, which they see as useful in the construction of feminine identities and communities.

Some radical feminists do see potential in digital forms of communication. Haraway argues that the anonymity granted by many forms of digital communication allows women to transcend their oppressed identity by taking on digital identities which avoid the negative judgements and stereotypes associated with femininity. She points out that in virtual communities like Second Life women can adopt 'cyborg identities' which are gender neutral or even experiment with masculine avatar identity.

Marxist feminists are generally pessimistic about the power of digital technology to change the lives of women for the better because, as Marxists, they believe that the ownership of digital technologies is in the hands of the capitalist class which is dominated by a masculine outlook. Capitalist companies are only interested in increasing profits. They are unlikely to invest in digital communication systems that rock the boat by questioning the nature of patriarchy. They are much more likely to invest in social networking sites such as Facebook or internet dating sites that reinforce traditional relations between the sexes.

Liberal feminists are the most optimistic about the power of digital communications to improve social conditions for women. They have actively used digital technology to empower women and to raise their consciousness about sexism, misogyny and patriarchy. For example, Laura Bates set up the Everyday Sexism project, which encourages women to share their experiences of sexism. Cochrane points out that other digital projects have focused on criticising the sexualisation of female children, violence against women and pornography. She argues that these projects have produced a new type of intersectional feminism in which women are now aware of how gender interacts with other forms of oppression such as class inequality, race, poverty, violence, religion and so on.

In conclusion, evidence suggests that women who use digital forms of communication may still be subjected to sexism, abuse and threats. Digital technology may have expanded the opportunities for feminists to put their case more widely and successfully but unfortunately misogynists are using such technology too.

**e** This is a well-argued, detailed answer with a good range and depth of knowledge about feminist views on digital forms of communication, supported with studies and contemporary examples. It is evaluative in tone and contrasts the strands of feminism, but evaluation could have been extended by challenging the feminist view from the perspective of other theoretical positions. **14/16 marks awarded (AO1 4/4, AO2 4/4, AO3 6/8).**

**Section B**

**4** Functionalists argue that education is clearly linked to the workplace. Durkheim suggests that in industrial societies a specialised division of labour is required, and that education can help produce a workforce with specialised skills to address this. During industrialisation, for example, literacy and numeracy became important in the workforce; this drove the expansion of compulsory education in the UK. Another functionalist view is that education helps in the process of role allocation. Davis and Moore suggest that in school we are sifted and sorted into appropriate roles for the workplace, based on our abilities and subject specialisms, which ensures that people with the right talents end up doing the right jobs.

While it's clear that the curriculum is linked to work more and more with the growth of vocational qualifications such as BTECs and GNVQs, many argue that the subjects learnt in school often have very little relevance in the world of work, and that the real link between education and the workplace is via the hidden curriculum suggested by Marxists. The most famous Marxist view on this comes from Bowles and Gintis. They discuss the correspondence principle, which is the idea that education closely corresponds to work, in that we learn to be motivated by external rewards such as exam results, and we learn the importance of things like discipline and hierarchy. All of these are necessary lessons we will take forward into the world of work. So we are learning how to be obedient and submissive workers for the benefit of capitalism. An alternative Marxist view comes from Willis, who argues that working-class boys learned to be bored and put up with school, skills they later needed to survive in their factory jobs.

So there are many ways in which education can be seen as linked to the workplace, and sociologists disagree on how the link works.

**ⓔ** A very good response outlining a range of ways in which education can be linked to the workplace. Slightly underdeveloped — the part on Willis could have been expanded, for example. **9/10 marks awarded (AO1 5/6, AO2 4/4).**

**5** In 1988 the Education Reform Act was passed by the Conservative government, influenced mainly by New Right principles of marketisation and competition. It included policies such as the National Curriculum, standardised testing and the publication of league tables. These were designed to increase parental choice, creating 'parentocracy', but it is questionable whether they increased equality of opportunity. The New Right would argue that allowing parents to access information about the performance of different schools and to choose which school to send their child to improved equality of opportunity, since all parents have access to the same information. Also, the National Curriculum meant that all schools taught the same content, so all students had equal opportunities in terms of what they learned.

These policies have been criticised, however, as not improving equal opportunities at all. Private schools don't have to follow the National Curriculum, which means not all students do study the same things. Also, parentocracy is rejected by social democrats and Marxists. Due to a lack of social and cultural capital, working-class parents may not be in a position to choose the best schools for their children. Gerwitz et al. describe middle-class parents as 'skilled choosers', but working-class parents are often 'disconnected choosers', who lack the skills and knowledge to use the system as effectively.

In the late 1990s and 2000s, some of New Labour's education policies were influenced by social democratic ideas and intended to improve equal opportunities. For example, Sure Start was a scheme to support preschool children from disadvantaged families, to avoid them falling behind before they started school. EAZs and EiC schemes also funded inner-city education authorities to provide extra services to schools in the poorest areas, and EMA was introduced to financially support students from disadvantaged backgrounds to allow them to stay on in education. All these policies aimed to bridge the gap between children from disadvantaged backgrounds and other children, to ensure they all got equal opportunities in school. It was hard to prove how effective they actually were, however, and these schemes have now been cut back or scrapped altogether.

Some New Labour policies did not seem to improve equality of opportunity at all. For example, although New Labour expanded university places, they also brought in tuition fees and further cuts to grants, meaning that opportunities to attend university were less equal.

The Coalition government brought in the 'pupil premium', which was an extra payment to schools for children on free school meals, which could be argued to improve equal opportunities by improving funding and facilities in schools in poorer areas. Other cuts, however, meant that this money did not make much difference, according to critics. Academies, introduced by New Labour but expanded by the Coalition, were also argued to improve equal opportunities, since they were originally set up to take over underperforming inner-city schools and bring in private funding to improve education for poorer children. Most secondary schools are now academies, however, and there is a big variation in their standards, with some doing worse than when they were run by local authorities. The current Conservative government has pushed for the further expansion of academies and free schools, which have even more independence. This can be seen as more about choice and marketisation than about improving equality of opportunity. The New Right may argue that the two go together, and that by raising standards for all schools using competition and market principles, all students will have more opportunities. Many would disagree, however, and the gap in attainment between children from the richest and the poorest backgrounds has not really changed, despite all the changes to education in the last 20–30 years.

**ⓔ** A range of policies is considered and the answer stays very well focused on the question. A good structure and debate is created by considering policies chronologically by the administration that introduced them. Some of the policies, such as EAZs/EiCs and EMA, could have been explained in a bit more detail. Evaluation is included throughout, though it is underdeveloped and lacking support in places. There is no separate conclusion, but the answer does end on a reflective note, which can be credited. **17/20 marks awarded (AO1 7/8, AO2 4/4, AO3 6/8).**

---

**6** There is a large attainment gap in terms of social class. For example, in 2011 just 34.6% of students eligible for free school meals, which is often used as a measure of deprivation, achieved 5 or more A* to C grades at GCSE including English and maths, compared to 62.0% of other students. In 2010, 77% of students with parents from higher professional backgrounds gained A-levels or equivalent, compared to 28% with parents from routine occupations. There are many competing explanations, including biological and cultural ones, but interactionists in particular argue that it is factors that happen within schools that provide the main explanation for these differences.

Teacher labelling is the main school factor to consider that interactionists believe in. Becker came up with labelling theory, arguing that a label based on a stereotype can be placed on someone and will affect the way they are treated. This label will then be internalised and become a master status, affecting everything that person does. It can also become a self-fulfilling prophecy, as the labelled person starts to accept the label and live up to it. Becker argued that labelling relates to power, and though we all label each other, some people have the power to make their labels stick. In terms of schools, teachers are the ones with the power and status to label students. Many interactionist studies have demonstrated this labelling process, including Hargreaves, who recognised the way that some labels can be positive, discussing the halo effect. Rosenthal and Jacobson also showed how positive labels can improve a student's progress in their famous study, where positively labelled students had made more progress after a year and continued to do so.

Many studies have applied these ideas to explain the differences in achievement according to social class. Becker argued that teachers have a perception of the 'ideal pupil' that fits with middle-class characteristics in terms of appearance, manner and behaviour. Rist found this in her study of an American kindergarten teacher. After only eight days, the teacher assigned the children to separate tables based on their perceived ability, but Rist found that social class was the underlying factor. The children seen as the fast learners, who were middle class, got the most attention and started to see themselves as smarter. On the other hand, the students on Table 3, who were from poorer backgrounds, eventually stopped participating and trying so hard. More recently these ideas have been supported by Dunne and Gazeley, who found that teachers judge children not just on ability, but on cultural assumptions relating to their social class. Most of the students that the teachers said were 'underachievers' also came from working-class backgrounds.

Hargreaves, and more recently Gillborn and Youdell, demonstrated how this class judgement can affect the sets students are put into more than their ability does. Teachers use these class-based assumptions to 'type' students. The sets students are put into will affect their achievement, as Keddie pointed out that children in lower sets are often denied access to knowledge, meaning they cannot achieve at the highest levels no matter what their effort levels.

Although there are lots of studies demonstrating teacher-labelling based on social class, this has been criticised as being too deterministic. There is evidence that some students will not accept the label, and will try to prove it wrong; this is known as the self-refuting prophecy. Also, functionalists would argue that it is individual and cultural factors that affect working-class students' achievement rather than teacher labelling. For example, Bernstein discusses how working-class students speak in a restricted code rather than the middle-class teachers' elaborated code. Arguments about cultural deprivation show that there might be other reasons for working-class students doing worse, which have nothing to do with school factors. These include parental support, norms and values, and cultural capital.

Other school factors could include the anti-school subcultures that form in schools, often as a response to teacher labelling and working-class feelings of disillusionment with education. Lacey argues that most Year 7 students arrive at secondary school with pro-school norms and values. The process of setting students by ability and often by social class, however, leads to a 'polarisation', where the top groups still have the pro-school subculture, but the bottom sets start to reject this. They become disenchanted with the whole thing, and start to develop anti-school subcultures in order to regain respect and status. Willis found that working-class boys formed anti-school subcultures that valued 'havin' a laff' and did not see academic achievement as desirable. Boys who are not part of this subculture may be bullied and pressured to join. Brown found that most working-class students just wanted to get by, however, and were not polarised into pro-school or anti-school. He identified three possible responses among the working-class students: 'getting in', where they wanted to join manual occupations; 'getting out', where they wanted to use education to get out of the working class; and 'getting on', where they just got on with it and did okay. Mac an Ghaill also suggests things may be less clear-cut, and that many working-class students had more complex attitudes towards school, not totally rejecting it. Evidence also suggests that these subcultures affect boys more than girls, and many girls may have anti-school subcultures but still be pro-education. But Jackson studied 'laddishness' in schools, and found evidence of this from both working-class boys and girls. It was quite cool to be clever, but not to work hard, and students hid from their friends the fact that they had revised or tried. This could be to avoid the appearance of weakness or failure.

A final school factor that may affect working-class underachievement is the 'hidden curriculum'. This is the term for the things you are taught in school that are not on the official National Curriculum, for example discipline, expectations and punctuality. Marxists such as Bowles and Gintis suggest that schools, through the hidden curriculum, brainwash children into their class position, and justify it with the illusion that school provides equal opportunities, making the working-class children believe they deserve to fail. Marxists would argue that schools are set up to ensure that working-class children do less well and that meritocracy is just a myth. This view is challenged by functionalists, who argue that schools do provide opportunities for all to succeed, and that if working-class students do less well it is cultural factors like their norms and values which cause it.

In conclusion, there are several school factors that can have an effect on students' achievement, including teacher labelling, student subcultures and the hidden curriculum. Clearly school factors do have a big effect on social class and achievement patterns.

ⓔ This answer has a very good range and depth of knowledge, considering various school factors, supported with evidence. There is some evaluation using alternative views and conflicting evidence, but this could have been developed. The conclusion was mainly summative — just repeating the main arguments rather than reflecting on their strength and reaching a reasoned view on how significant these factors may be. This affects the evaluation (AO3) marks. **34/40 marks awarded (AO1 15/16, AO2 8/8, AO3 11/16).**

ⓔ **Overall, the student scored 92 marks out of the 105 available.**

# Question 3

Section A

*Globalisation and the digital social world*

**Read the source material and answer all the questions in Section A.**

**Source A**

A Glasgow University study led by Heather Cleland Woods in 2015 questioned more than 460 teenagers at a secondary school in Scotland about their general social media habits, and in particular their night-time use of sites such as Facebook and Twitter. The researchers concluded that teenagers who engage with social media during the night are increasing their risk of mental health problems such as anxiety and depression. The research found that many pupils felt they had to be available on social media 24/7 and worried about what would happen if they did not respond immediately to texts or posts or did not 'like' their friends' posts on Facebook and Instagram. Girls in particular worried about the consequences of not conforming to these digital pressures, especially the online bullying.

> **Source B**
>
> Sherry Turkle argues that Twitter and Facebook do not connect people. Rather they isolate them from reality. She claims that digital technology is threatening to dominate our lives and make us less human. It creates the illusion that it allows people to communicate better and to gain social capital but it is actually isolating its users from real human interactions in a cyber-reality that is a poor imitation of the real world. However, many commentators defend social media. They point out that e-mails, Twitter and Facebook have led to more communication, not less — especially for people who may have trouble meeting in the real world because of great distance or social difference.

1   With reference to the sources, explain how engaging with digital social networks may have negative consequences for young people.  [9 marks]

ⓔ You must make clear reference to at least one of the sources as well as your wider knowledge.

2   With reference to the sources, discuss the view that developments in digital communities have positively affected the quality of social relationships.  [10 marks]

ⓔ You need to supplement reference to at least one of the sources with your wider knowledge. The phrase 'discuss' means you are expected to include some ideas and evidence both for and against the statement. Remember to reach a brief conclusion.

3   Outline and evaluate Marxist views on developments in digital communications.  [16 marks]

ⓔ Identify the key aspects of the theory and then explain them. Evaluation requires discussion of both strengths and weaknesses.

## Section B

**Answer all the questions in Section B.**

*Education*

4   Outline evidence that demonstrates global disparities in educational provision.  [10 marks]

ⓔ Try to include a range of evidence in this type of question, which may include statistics and examples. Remember, you don't need to evaluate but might include some competing views if appropriate.

5   To what extent are cultural factors responsible for educational inequality in relation to gender?  [20 marks]

ⓔ Cultural factors may be interpreted to include norms and values learnt in the family, but also from peer groups and subcultures, as well as wider cultural norms. The phrase 'to what extent' requires you to consider evidence that supports the idea, but also evidence that challenges it.

**6** Outline and assess the view that education operates in the interests of the ruling class. [40 marks]

ⓔ If you are given a 'view' to assess that does not specifically mention the name of a theory, it is important to identify which theory or theories may hold this view and which would disagree, so that your answer can stay well focused on the question.

---

**Student answer**

### Section A

**1** Young people are the most frequent users of social media and they often take a great deal of care in how they package and present themselves online. Research shows that they may exaggerate the more socially attractive aspects of their personality and not mention less cool or geeky aspects such as the fact they are A-grade students or that they like school. This can put great pressure on young people socially, and they will constantly be comparing themselves to others. There is evidence that teenage obsession with their virtual identity means they are more 'me-centred' than previous generations and this is producing more moodiness and anxiety.

The effect on time use is also a concern. Source A shows that if teenagers are always checking social media when they should be asleep this will cause mental health problems such as anxiety and depression. The study also found that girls were worried about the consequences of not conforming to online pressure to respond to other people's texts or to 'like' what their friends had posted. They were very worried about the possibility of online bullying.

Brignall discusses 'current cyber-youth' who have grown up with the internet as an important part of their everyday life, and argues that due to the pervasive use of the internet, there has been a decrease in face-to-face interaction among youth, which might have consequences for their social skills and self-concept, and lead to social isolation and a loss of privacy.

Supporting Brignall's concerns, some sociologists have suggested online interaction has reduced face-to-face interaction. This may mean that a teenager may be friend-rich online but may feel isolated and lonely because they rarely spend time in the physical company of other teenagers.

---

ⓔ This answer looks at a range of factors quoting Source A and using Brignall's ideas. However, it is less successful in using a range of sociological research and concepts, and leaves some points somewhat vague and unsubstantiated, thus not quite giving enough detail for full marks. **8/9 marks awarded (AO1 4/5, AO2 4/4).**

---

**2** There is a big debate as to whether developments in digital communication have improved human interaction and relationships or whether they have worsened them. Those who argue in favour say that digital connections have brought about a participatory culture. For example, Source B says that e-mails, texting, Twitter, Facebook and other forms of social media have led to more communication and expanded people's network of relationships. In the past people may have lost contact with people when they moved to other parts of the country. Social differences may have prevented people meeting others. However, social media such as Facebook transcend both distance and social difference, having a positive effect on social relationships.

Van Dijk sees a number of advantages in social media connections. In particular, he argues that it produces various types of social capital which can be shared and reciprocated by others such as 'bonding capital', which refers to the opportunities for mutual aid provided by people with similar interests or bonds to one another. For example, an A-level sociology student might go online to ask a community of other A-level sociology students for revision materials. Bridging social capital refers to resources that might be shared among people who are very different to one another, for example feminists may use Twitter and discover that they have a great deal in common with other political causes and as a result construct online political alliances with groups such as vegans or environmentalists.

Another advantage of social networking is that it functions to micro-coordinate activity among friends and relatives especially if they are separated by distance. It may provide a social lifeline for those who are isolated, shy or disabled. It may provide a voice for groups denied a platform in traditional media such as minority groups.

However, as Source B indicates, some sociologists believe that social networking has created a new set of problems for society. Turkle believes that social networking does not connect people because online relationships are superficial and weak. She argues that online relationships diminish the value of true friendship because they lack intimacy, vulnerability and physical closeness. Turkle goes as far in Source B as to suggest that social networks isolate their participants from reality and that they are a poor imitation of the real world. For example, she argues that people are constantly on their phones checking for texts and social network updates. She argues that this is unhealthy because it produces anxiety and when people misplace their phones, they feel cut off from reality. Finally, some critics of social networking claim that it has coarsened young people's attitudes. It is claimed that online they are more selfish, meaner and narcissistic than they are in person. As a result, online bullying, sexting and sexual harassment have become more common, as mentioned in Source A.

In conclusion, it is clear there are both positive and negative effects on social relationships, which very much depend on how digital communication is used, so it can be a tool for extending relationships, but can also have isolating effects.

**e** This response uses Source B well, but also goes beyond this, identifying a range of views. It is focused and relevant material is applied to the question. **10/10 marks awarded (AO1 4/4, AO2 2/2, AO3 4/4).**

**3** Marxists argue that global processes involved in the spread of digital communications are merely an extension of the ongoing globalisation process, driven by capitalism. The development of digital forms of communication has greatly contributed to capitalism's search for greater profits.

Additionally, Marxists have suggested that capitalism is guilty of cultural imperialism. Marcuse argued that global culture was characterised by cultural homogeneity or sameness. He claimed that this was unsurprising seeing that popular culture was mainly transmitted by a handful of American cultural corporations such as Disney. Updating these ideas to reflect digital media, McChesney has made similar observations about the similarity of digital content and social networking. Facebook, Google and Twitter, for example, operate in hundreds of countries across the world. He claims companies like Facebook, Google and Twitter are like imperial powers colonising the minds of millions of people across the world so they behave and think in the same predictable way. McChesney argues that this 'cult of homogeneity' destroys cultural diversity by crowding out local cultural products. Marxists also dislike cultural homogeneity because they believe that it has the ideological effect of promoting consumption (the lifeblood of capitalism) and encouraging conformity. It results in false class consciousness as people are distracted from thinking critically about issues such as inequality.

Marxists are also very critical about the uses of digital communications and social media because they believe that they are ideological in that they function on behalf of the capitalist ruling class to reproduce and justify class inequality. Marxists believe that the role of digital social media such as Facebook functions to reinforce false class consciousness because such networks mainly focus on non-critical issues such as identity, entertainment and consumption, and consequently are rarely important vehicles of protest and social change. Marxists believe that those who own or control these social networks aim to manipulate how people think and to ensure they only get a narrow range of 'approved' views and knowledge. Marxists point out that most of the internet's content is controlled by a handful of media conglomerates which have a vested commercial interest in encouraging people to consume rather than criticise. Fuchs argues that corporations and the governments they support exert greater power on social networks than ordinary people and they may use that power to silence or mute those who are too critical of capitalism.

Another concern Marxists may express is the power of digital media to monitor and control ordinary people, as evidenced by Edward Snowden's revelations. So digital media may be seen as yet another form of control, both direct and indirect, linking to Althusser's ideas of the repressive and ideological state apparatus.

However, Marxists assume that providers of digital forms of communication are united in promoting a single ideology, but they are not because they are competing with one another for profit. If their companies are pushing capitalist ideology this is most likely an accidental product of competition.

Additionally, not all Marxists agree that digital media always work in the interests of the capitalist class. Castells, for instance, takes a much more positive view, arguing that digital media can revitalise democracy by giving a voice to muted oppressed groups. Some argue that social media actually empowers people, and prevents the ideology of the powerful from dominating, since opposing, and even revolutionary, views can be spread more easily. The Arab Spring revolutions are often cited as an example of the power that social media has to spread dissenting ideas.

In conclusion, it is unsurprising that Marxists may express concern about the ideological control of digital media, given its power in today's society. However, more optimistic commentators have recognised the lack of control the powerful have in terms of social media — for example, with the rise of citizen journalism and user-generated content, although the divide between the digital 'haves' and 'have nots' needs to be bridged for this to be effective.

**e** This answer shows excellent knowledge of the Marxist perspective, with supporting studies and examples. There is some attempt to evaluate, however this could have gone further to explore a greater range of counterviews, such as feminist and postmodernist ideas. **15/16 marks awarded (AO1 4/4, AO2 4/4, AO3 7/8).**

## Section B

4  Globally there is a lot of inequality in educational provision. In the richer Western countries education tends to be compulsory at least into the teenage years, and also free to access, whereas in less economically developed countries educational provision tends to be patchier.

The World Inequality Database on Education (WIDE) shows that in some of the poorest countries, like Chad and Somalia, nearly 90% of the poorest children have never attended school. Even children in these countries who do go to school are often in education for less than four years in total, and take-up for higher education is very low. The situation is worst in rural areas due to access issues, but also because many children from the poorest families are relied on to work for the family. There is also a shortage of trained teachers and facilities. For older students, participation in higher education globally is increasing towards 50% in many countries, whereas in sub-Saharan Africa the participation rate is just 7%, and this would only be the wealthiest groups. Filmer argues that poverty is the most important issue holding children back. This can be a vicious circle, since for poorer countries having an uneducated workforce could be a barrier to further economic development.

Differences in educational provision don't just make a difference between developed and less developed economies. The Programme for International Student Assessment (PISA) assesses performances of 15-year-olds in areas like reading, maths and problem-solving across 65 different countries that mostly have developed economies and compulsory education. It shows a large difference in performance. In 2012, the UK came 23rd for reading and 26th for maths, and the USA did even worse. Asian countries tended to be the top performers. Differences accounting for this may be cultural attitudes towards education, but there are also differences in the length of the school day, the style of teaching and the curriculum, which may have an impact. For example, in South Korea, which scores highly in PISA tests, it is common for children to do a 'double-shift' of school and extra tuition, studying for more than ten hours per day.

Overall, though, it is clear that children in the developed countries in general enjoy much higher standards of and access to educational provision than those in the poorest countries.

ⓔ This answer considers several different issues in terms of inequality of educational provision, including access to schooling, access to higher education and types of provision, which gives it good range. Evidence from global organisations, statistics and examples are all creditable as sociological exvidence, especially given the lack of named studies relating to this topic, so despite a slight lack of substantiation, this answer has enough range and depth for full marks. **10/10 marks awarded (AO1 6/6, AO2 4/4).**

**5**  Gender inequality in education is quite complex. In terms of achievement, girls are doing better than boys, but there are other issues such as subject choice where girls could be seen to have inequality. Different reasons for these inequalities have been put forward, including school factors, but some argue that cultural factors make the most difference.

Since the 1990s girls have achieved higher at GCSE and at A-level than boys in most subjects. Before this it was the other way round, however. One of the main arguments to explain this is changing cultural attitudes towards females. Due to the feminist movement in the 1960s and '70s, ideas about gender equality became more accepted, and girls in education in the 1990s grew up with more positive role models and mothers whose attitudes reflected these ideas. Sharpe found that when she interviewed schoolgirls in the 1970s they had low aspirations, and their priorities were to get married and have children. When she repeated this with girls in the 1990s, however, she found that they wanted to do well academically, and saw themselves as more likely to have careers. Francis and Skelton more recently found that girls all saw their futures in terms of a career rather than seeing marriage and family as their main goal. This cultural change could be a reason for the changes in girls' achievements.

At the same time as this, males have faced a crisis of masculinity according to Mac an Ghaill. Many boys are now growing up in lone-parent families led by mothers and may lack male-breadwinner role models. As many working-class traditional male industries have declined, laddism and more aggressive male behaviour has become a way of asserting masculinity. This may lead to boys forming hyper-masculine subcultures, which are often anti-school. Mac an Ghaill studied the macho lads, who valued the '3 Fs' (fighting, f***ing and football) over academic achievement. Whereas girls have realised that they need to do well academically to be independent and successful in the job market, Francis argues that many boys have unrealistic attitudes (about becoming footballers, for example) that do not inspire them to work hard at school. Archer and Yamashita found that boys had anti-school and anti-education attitudes, valuing their 'bad boy' image, and seeing reading and academic qualifications as 'soft'. Working hard was not seen as masculine, and they demonstrated 'hyper-heterosexuality' within their subculture.

This suggests that subcultural pressures are encouraging boys to try less hard in school, whereas changing cultural attitudes are doing the opposite for girls, which explains the differences in achievement. Jackson found that some working-class girls also formed anti-school subcultures, however, that showed similar attitudes to the boys. She called these girls 'ladettes'. Therefore, social class may be the issue rather than gender, since boys from middle-class backgrounds continue to do well and don't tend to form anti-school subcultures. Additionally, boys from Chinese and Indian backgrounds are performing very well in school, so ethnicity is also a factor.

There may also be other explanations for the gender differences in achievement. The feminisation of the curriculum could lead to gender inequality. This includes the introduction of coursework, which favours girls, and the lack of male teachers within schools, especially at primary level, which may give boys less to relate to in school. Teacher labelling may be another reason. Though Skelton and Francis found that boys tend to dominate spaces and attention at school, Mitsos and Brown suggest that teachers have higher academic expectations of girls.

Another aspect of gender inequality relates to subject choice, and girls still tend to choose arts and humanities subjects, which are often seen as 'soft' subjects and may lead to less high status careers, often in the caring professions, affecting pay. Males, despite doing worse academically, still dominate sciences and engineering. These differences can be seen as cultural, to do with gender socialisation in the family and role models in the media. Whether girls should be encouraged to take science-related courses is debatable, however, and some feminists argue that a more relevant questions to ask is why the professions dominated by females have lower status and lower pay in the first place.

In conclusion, gender inequalities in education have clear links to cultural factors, both in wider society and within subcultures. It should be remembered, however, that achievement for both genders is increasing, and the gap is narrowing. Other factors such as class and ethnicity may also be significant when considering educational inequality, so the extent to which cultural factors influence gender inequality is open to question.

**e** This is an extremely well-focused answer that covers a range of cultural factors in relation to boys and girls in detail. Coming at a question from different angles is a good way to add range. There is an evaluative tone all the way through, and a well-reasoned conclusion, though AO3 is the slightly weaker skill here. **18/20 marks awarded (AO1 8/8, AO2 4/4, AO3 6/8).**

**6** The view that education operates in the interests of the ruling class comes from Marxists, who argue that education is part of the superstructure that supports capitalism. Many would disagree, however, and functionalists would argue that education operates in the interests of the whole society.

Althusser argued that in order to maintain control over the proletariat, the bourgeoisie use the repressive state apparatus, which is control by force using the police, the criminal justice system and the army, for example. It is much more effective to gain ideological control, however, and the ideological state apparatuses do this, controlling people's ideas and preventing them from realising the need to rebel. Education is one of the ISA and it transmits capitalist ideology in a way people don't even realise. Schools don't encourage critical thinking or any challenge to the system; they encourage all children to grow up accepting capitalist ideas and believing that the system of sorting people into different classes is fair. This could be challenged, however, since many subjects, especially social sciences, do encourage critical thinking.

In support of Althusser's ideas, American Marxists Bowles and Gintis see the education system as a 'giant myth-making machine' that legitimises inequality and brainwashes children into accepting their place in the capitalist system. They say that school corresponds with work, and that at school children are learning how to be obedient and submissive workers. At school, you learn the importance of hierarchy and that some people are more important than others. You learn about discipline and punishment as well as external rewards. All these things link to work within the capitalist system, so workers will accept orders from their superiors in the hierarchy at work and accept their pay packet as their reward. Bowles and Gintis argue that the functionalist idea of meritocracy — that you get what you deserve based on your talent and effort — is a myth that is promoted through the hidden curriculum in schools. By making us believe that we deserve our exam results, it stops us challenging our future class position and low wages, and so we don't see that the system is stacked against the working class from the start. From these two famous Marxist arguments it can definitely be seen that education operates in the interests of the ruling class.

These ideas are challenged by functionalists, however. They would point to the fact that education is free and accessible to everyone in the UK and that many working-class children do succeed and go on to university and into well-paid jobs. Rather than legitimising inequality and keeping everyone in their place, education actually allows hard-working and talented students to succeed whatever their background, and is a driver of social mobility. Additionally, it is important, according to Davis and Moore, to sort people based on ability so that we have the right people in the right jobs. That is functional for everyone. Therefore education does not just work in the interests of the ruling class, but in the interests of everyone.

Another criticism of Marxism is that its ideas are outdated. The days when children from state schools all ended up in manual jobs, while private school students went to the top universities and got the top jobs are arguably a thing of the past. Evidence from the Sutton Trust, however, suggests that private school students still dominate the professions, so maybe Marxist ideas are not that outdated. The Marxist Rikowski would agree with this. In contemporary society, with globalisation and the growth of multinational companies, capitalism is stronger than ever and the ruling class's grip on these powerful companies is growing. Rikowski argues that capitalism and market forces have been brought into the education system, replacing any meritocratic ideals, and that education will inevitably become more results-driven, and operate even more in the interests of the ruling class. The expansion of academies and free schools, and the focus on parentocracy and league tables, are all trends that support Rikowski's views. In a free-market environment, education is even more likely to operate just in the interests of the ruling class. The New Right would disagree, however, and argue that these changes will drive up standards for all students, so they are in everyone's interests.

Another Marxist view comes from Bourdieu. He argues that middle-class parents have more cultural capital, which advantages their children in education, meaning that there is not a level playing field in schools. He argues that the main aim of education is cultural reproduction, which means that the culture of the ruling class is passed on to the next generation of workers. By giving more status to the cultural knowledge associated with the ruling class, working-class students are taught that their culture is inferior — their failure is therefore justified. Culture also plays a large part in higher education, disadvantaging students from working-class backgrounds. In the top universities, middle-class students will be like a 'fish in water' according to Bourdieu, having already attended private schools, whereas many state school students feel like a 'fish out of water' even if they get into one of the top universities, since it is so alien to their culture. Bourdieu's ideas can be challenged, however, as the school curriculum moves away from the more traditional forms of learning, and more and more university students do come from ordinary backgrounds.

A final view that comes from a Marxist perspective, but that challenges other Marxists such as Bowles and Gintis, comes from Paul Willis. In some ways he would agree that the education system operates in the interests of the ruling class, but he disagrees about how it works in practice. He studied working-class boys in a comprehensive school who had a very realistic attitude towards school, as something to be endured by 'havin' a laff' and messing around. The boys did not value academic qualifications, and did not learn how to become submissive workers as Bowles and Gintis argued. The lads were resisting the capitalist system and understood that the education system was unfair, and they refused to be obedient and accept the teachers' authority. By adopting these anti-school attitudes, however, the boys did end up failing academically and spending their lives in local factory, and so the school did turn out workers and benefit the ruling class in the end.

In conclusion, there are convincing Marxist arguments suggesting that the education system does operate in the interests of the ruling class, by reproducing social class inequalities. As many working-class students have found, however, it can also benefit students from all backgrounds, and the existence of subjects like sociology, which encourages students to think critically about their education, could be used to question the Marxist view.

**e** Excellent knowledge and understanding of a wide range of Marxist ideas is shown. It is important in a question like this to stay focused on the view in the question and to resist the temptation to describe alternative views at length. This answer manages to do this effectively, using the wording in the question frequently to show the relevance of points made and not getting side-tracked. Evaluation is sustained and there is a well-reasoned conclusion. Though more evaluation is possible, it would be hard to improve on this in the time available so it would be awarded full marks. **40/40 marks awarded (AO1 16/16, AO2 8/8, AO3 16/16).**

**e** **Overall, the student scored 101 marks out of the 105 available.**

## Knowledge check answers

1 The distances between physical places are becoming easier to reach due to better transport and time is becoming shortened through instantaneous messaging, for example.

2 Advances in digital forms of communication and computer technology; ownership and control of world digital media being concentrated in the hands of a few; rapid growth in travel and mass tourism.

3 In the twenty-first century people are more likely to be organised into horizontal digital communication networks using new forms of social media, so that all people believing in a religion communicate at the same level. This is in contrast to the traditional vertical organisations of the past where you were more likely to communicate with people of a similar level to yourself. For example, the congregation would communicate in a less democratic way; there was less access to people in more senior positions in the Church.

4 That they are created by the middle class, who seek to reinforce capitalist ideology.

5 They are the same as before but speed of transmission is much greater, giving the impression they have changed.

6 The economically repressed are unable to have a voice as they are repressed by digital media owners.

7 They both perpetuate patriarchy.

8 Men and their masculine culture.

9 A form of feminism adopted by many younger women who are becoming aware of a number of forms of and causes of oppression and how they may intersect with gender.

10 The net generation refers to the first generation that experienced and used the internet in the 1990s, while the iGeneration refers to those born after 2000.

11 Regional disparities; smartphones less used; only 7% online.

12 Boellstorff found that people are able to reshape their identity and experiment with it. Carter found that people's on- and offline identity was seen as equally important.

13 Socially desirable, fictitious and using identity performance.

14 Bonding; bridging; political.

15 Being online together but without any emotionally meaningful connection.

16 Facebook was used in Egypt to schedule public protests but Curran argues that the Arab Spring was caused by deep-seated economic, political and religious factors.

17 It combines Hollywood culture and Indian culture to produce something new.

18 The three key roles of education according to functionalists are to create a specialised division of labour, to act as a bridge between the family and education, and effective role allocation.

19 The three key roles of education according to Marxists are to preserve capitalism through maintaining a ruling class ideology, to create a 'myth of meritocracy', and to prepare an obedient workforce.

20 The key similarity between the social democratic and New Right approaches is that education should meet the needs of the economy.

21 The main Marxist criticism of vocational education is that it is exploitative of the young people on the training schemes as they are used as cheap labour and gain little from it.

22 The main outside and in-school factors relating to class and achievement are cultural, material and speech codes, labelling/self-fulfilling prophecy, and setting.

23 The main outside and in-school factors relating to ethnicity and achievement are cultural and material factors, labelling/self-fulfilling prophecy, institutional racism and setting.

24 The main outside and in-school factors relating to gender and achievement are changing attitudes, changing landscapes, subject choice and in-school changes.

25 Education was first measured globally in 2000 by UNESCO.

26 The comprehensive system largely replaced the tripartite system (the final ban on the creation of new grammar schools came in the Schools Standards and Framework Act 1998).

27 The two main ideological political influences are New Right and social democratic.

28 The four main aims of governments in relation to educational policy since 1988 have been: raising standards; equality of opportunity; meeting the needs of the economy; creating diversity and choice.

# Index

Note: Key words are denoted by **bold** page numbers.

# Index